Enid

GW00361653

THE
ENCHANTED
WOOD

Sorcha
Aobh
Reynolds

Sorcha ☺

Enid Blyton

THE
ENCHANTED
WOOD

DEAN

EGMONT

We bring stories to life

First published in Great Britain 1939 by Newnes
This edition published 2012 by Dean,
an imprint of Egmont UK Limited
The Yellow Building, 1 Nicholas Road, London W11 4AN

Text copyright © 1939 Hodder and Stoughton Ltd.
Illustration copyright © 2012 Hodder and Stoughton Ltd.
Enid Blyton © 2012 Hodder and Stoughton Ltd.
All rights reserved.

ISBN 978 0 6035 6815 2
1 3 5 7 9 10 8 6 4 2
43538/6

A CIP catalogue record for this title is
available from the British Library

Printed and bound in Great Britain

All rights reserved. No part of this publication may be
reproduced, stored in a retrieval system, or transmitted,
in any form or by any means, electronic, mechanical,
photocopying, recording or otherwise, without the prior
permission of the publisher and copyright owner.

CONTENTS

CONTENTS continued

I. HOW THEY FOUND
THE MAGIC WOOD

There were once three children, called Joe, Beth and Frannie. All their lives they had lived in a town, but now their father had a job in the country, so they were all to move as soon as they possibly could.

'What fun to be in the country!' said Joe. 'I shall learn all about animals and birds!'

'And I shall pick as many flowers as I want to,' said Beth.

'And I shall have a garden of my own,' said Frannie.

When the day came for the move all the children were excited. A small van came to their door and two men helped their father and mother to pile everything into it. When it was full the van drove away, and the children put on their coats and hats to go with their mother to catch a train to the station.

'Now we're off!' cried Joe.

'The country, the country!' sang Beth.

'We might see fairies there!' said Frannie.

The train whistled, and chuffed out of the station. The children pressed their noses to the window and watched the dirty houses and the chimneys race by. How they hated the town! How lovely it would be to be in the clean country, with flowers growing everywhere, and birds singing in the hedges!

'We might have adventures in the country,' said Joe. 'There will be streams and hillsides, big fields and dark woods. Oooh, it will be lovely!'

'You won't have any more adventures in the country than you will have in the town,' said their father. 'I dare say you will find it all very dull.'

But that's where he was quite wrong. My goodness, the things that happened to those three children!

They arrived at last at the tiny station where they were to get out. A sleepy-looking porter put their two bags on a trolley, and said he would bring them along later. Off they all went down the winding country lane, chattering loudly.

'I wonder if we've got a garden?' said Frannie.

But before they reached their new home they were tired out and could not bother to say a word more to each other. Their cottage was five miles from the station, and as the children's father could not afford to do anything but walk there, it seemed a very long way indeed. There was no bus to take them, so the tired children dragged their feet along, wishing for a glass of warm milk and a cosy bed.

At last they got there – and dear me, it was worth all the walk, for the cottage was sweet. Roses hung from the walls – red and white and pink – and honeysuckle was all round the front door. It was lovely!

The van was at the door, and the two men were moving all the furniture into the little house. Father helped, whilst Mother went to light the kitchen stove to make them all a hot drink.

They were so tired that they could do nothing but drink hot milk, eat some toast and tumble into their roughly-made beds. Joe looked out of the window but he was too sleepy to see properly. In one minute the two girls in their small room were asleep, and Joe too, in his even tinier room.

What fun it was to wake up in the morning and see the sun shining in at strange windows! It didn't take Joe, Beth and Frannie very long to dress. Then they were out in the little garden, running through the grass that had grown so long, and smelling the roses that grew all around.

Mother had cooked eggs for them, and they ate their breakfast hungrily.

'It's lovely to be in the country!' said Joe, looking out of the window to the far-away hills.

'We can grow vegetables in the garden,' said Beth.

'There will be glorious walks all round,' said Frannie.

That day everyone helped to get the little house straight and tidy. Father was going to work the next

day. Mother hoped there would be someone to give her washing to do, then she would make enough money to buy a few hens. That would be lovely!

'I shall collect the eggs each morning and evening,' said Frannie happily.

'Let's go out and see what the country round about is like,' said Joe. 'Can you spare us for an hour, Mother?'

'Yes, run along,' said Mother. So off the three children went, out of the tiny white front gate and into the lane.

They explored all round about. They ran across a field where pink clover was full of bees. They paddled in a small brown stream that chattered away to itself under the willow trees in the sunshine.

And then they suddenly came to the wood. It was not far from their cottage, at the back. It looked quite an ordinary wood, except that the trees were a darker green than usual. A narrow ditch separated the wood from the overgrown lane.

'A wood!' said Beth, in delight. 'We shall be able to have picnics here!'

'It's rather a mysterious sort of wood,' said Joe thoughtfully. 'Don't you think so, Beth?'

'Well, the trees are rather thick, but they seem about the same as any others,' said Beth.

'They don't quite,' said Frannie. 'The noise the leaves make is different. Listen!'

They listened – and Frannie was right. The leaves of the trees in the wood did not rustle in quite the same way as other trees nearby did.

'It's almost as if they were really talking to one

another,' said Beth. 'Whispering secrets – real secrets, that we just can't understand.'

'It's a magic wood!' said Frannie suddenly.

Nobody said anything. They stood and listened. 'Wisha-wisha-wisha-wisha-wisha!' said the trees in the wood, and bent towards one another in a friendly way.

'There might be fairy-folk in there,' said Beth. 'Shall we jump over the ditch and go in?'

'No,' said Joe. 'We might get lost. Let's find our way around before we go into big woods like this.'

'Joe! Beth! Frannie!' suddenly came their mother's voice from the cottage not far off. 'It's time for lunch, time for lunch!'

The children felt hungry all at once. They forgot the strange wood and ran back to their new home. Mother had new bread with strawberry jam for them, and they ate a whole loaf between them.

Father came in as they were finishing. He had been shopping for Mother in the village three miles away and he was hungry and tired.

'We've been exploring everywhere, Father!' said Beth, pouring him out a big cup of tea.

'We've found a lovely wood,' said Joe. 'The trees really seem to be talking to one another, Father.'

'That must be the wood I've heard about this afternoon,' said Father. 'It has a strange name, children.'

'What is it called?' asked Joe.

'It's called the Enchanted Wood,' said their father. 'People don't go there if they can help it. It's funny to hear things like this nowadays, and I don't expect there is really anything strange about the wood. But just be careful not to go too far into it, in case you get lost.'

The children looked in excitement at one another. The Enchanted Wood! What a lovely name!

And each child secretly thought the same thought – 'I shall go and explore the Enchanted Wood as soon as ever I can!'

Their father set them to work in the overgrown garden once they had finished their meal. Joe had to pull up the tough thistles and the two girls had to weed the untidy vegetable bed. They spoke to one another in joyful voices.

'The Enchanted Wood! We knew there was something magical about it!'

'I guessed there were fairies there!' said Frannie.

'We'll do some more exploring as soon as we can!' cried Beth. 'We'll find out what those whispering trees are saying! We'll know all the secrets of the wood before many weeks are past!'

And that night, at bedtime, all three stood at the window, looking out on the dark, whispering wood behind the cottage. What would they find in the Enchanted Wood?

II. FIRST VISIT TO THE WOOD

The three children had no chance to visit the Enchanted Wood until the next week, because they had to help their mother and father all they could. There was the garden to get tidy, clothes and kitchen things to be unpacked and put away, and a great deal of cleaning to be done.

Sometimes Joe was free and could have gone by himself. Sometimes the girls were sent out for a walk, but Joe was busy. None of them wanted to go without the others, so they had to wait. And then at last their chance came.

'You can have your lunch outdoors today,' said Mother. 'You've worked well, all of you, and you deserve a picnic. I'll cut you some sandwiches, and you can take along some nice fresh milk.'

'We'll go to the Wood!' whispered Beth to the others, and with excited faces and beating hearts they helped their mother to pack their picnic into a big basket.

They set off. There was a small gate at the bottom of their back garden that led into the overgrown lane running by the wood. They unlatched the gate and stood in the lane. They could see the trees in the wood, and hear them talking their strange tree-talk: 'Wisha-wisha-wisha-wisha!'

'I feel as if there are adventures about,' said Joe.

'Come on! Over the ditch we go – and into the Enchanted Wood!'

One by one the children jumped over the narrow ditch. They stood beneath the trees and peered about. Small freckles of sunshine lay here and there on the ground, but not very many, for the trees were so thick. It was dim and green there, and a small bird nearby sang an odd little song over and over again.

'It really *is* magic!' said Frannie suddenly. 'I can feel magic about somewhere, can't you, Beth? Can't you, Joe?'

'Yes,' said the others, and their eyes shone with excitement. 'Come on!'

They went down a little green path that looked as if it had been made for rabbits, it was so small and narrow.

'Don't let's go too far,' said Joe. 'We had better wait till we know the paths a bit better before we go deep into the wood. Look about for a place to sit down and have our sandwiches, girls.'

'I can see some wild strawberries!' cried Beth, and she knelt down and pressed back some pretty leaves, showing the others deep red strawberries below.

'Let's pick some and have them with our picnic too,' said Frannie. So they picked hard, and soon had enough to make a fine meal.

'Let's sit down under that old oak tree over there,' said Joe. 'It's all soft moss beneath. It will be like sitting on a green velvet cushion.'

So they sat down, and unpacked their sandwiches. Soon they were munching away happily, listening to the dark green leaves overhead saying 'Wisha-wisha' all the time.

And it was whilst they were in the middle of their picnic that they saw a very peculiar thing. Frannie noticed it first.

Not far off was a clear piece of soft grass. As Frannie looked at it she noticed bumps appearing on it. She stared in surprise. The bumps grew. The earth rose up and broke in about six places.

'Look!' said Frannie, in a low voice, pointing to the piece of grass. 'What's happening over there?'

All three of them watched in silence. And then they saw what it was. Six big toadstools were growing quickly up from the ground, pushing their way through, and rising up steadily!

'I've never seen *that* happen before!' said Joe, in astonishment.

'Shh!' said Beth. 'Don't make a noise. I can hear footsteps.'

The others listened. Sure enough they heard the sound of pattering feet and little high voices.

'Let's get behind a bush – quickly,' said Beth suddenly. 'Whoever it is that is coming will be frightened if they see us. There's magic happening here, and we want to see it!'

They scrambled up and crept quietly behind a thick bush, taking their basket with them. They hid just in time, for even as Beth settled down and parted the leaves of the bush to peep through, there came a troop of small men with long beards almost reaching the ground!

'Elves!' whispered Joe.

The elves went to the toadstools and sat down on

them. They were holding a meeting. One of them had a bag with him which he put down behind his toadstool. The children could not hear what was being said, but they heard the sound of the chattering voices, and caught one or two words.

Suddenly Joe nudged Beth and Frannie. He had seen something else. The girls saw it too. An ugly, gnome-like fellow was creeping up silently behind the meeting on the toadstools. None of the elves saw him or heard him.

'He's after that bag!' whispered Joe. And so he was! He reached out a long arm. His bony fingers closed on the bag. He began to draw it away under a bush.

Joe jumped up. He was not going to watch people being robbed without saying something! He shouted loudly:

'Stop thief! Hey, look at that gnome behind you!'

In a fright the elves all leapt up. The gnome jumped to his feet and sped off with the bag. The elves stared after him in dismay, not one of them following him. The robber ran towards the children's bush. He didn't know they were there.

As quick as lightning Joe put out his foot and tripped up the running gnome. Down he went, crash! The bag flew from his hand and Beth picked it up and threw it to the astonished elves, who were still standing by the toadstools. Joe tried to grab the gnome – but he was up and off like a bird.

The children tore after him. In between the trees they went, dodging here and there – and at last they saw the gnome leap up to the low branches of a great tree, and pull himself into the leaves. The children sank down at the bottom, out of breath.

'We've got him now!' said Joe. 'He can't get down without being caught!'

'Here are the elves coming,' said Beth, wiping her hot forehead. The little bearded men ran up and bowed.

'You are very good to us,' said the biggest one. 'Thank you for saving our bag. We have valuable papers in there.'

'We've got the gnome for you too,' said Joe, as he pointed up into the tree. 'He went up there. If you surround the tree and wait, you will be able to catch him as he comes down.'

But the elves would not come too near the tree. They looked half frightened of it.

'He will not come down until he wants to,' said the biggest elf. 'That is the oldest and most magic tree in the world. It is the Faraway Tree.'

'The Faraway Tree!' said Beth, in wonder. 'What an odd name! Why do you call it that?'

'It's a very strange tree,' said another elf. 'Its top

reaches the far-away places in a way we don't understand. Sometimes its top branches may be in Witchland, sometimes in lovely countries, sometimes in peculiar places that no one has ever heard of. We never climb it because we never know what might be at the top!'

'How very strange!' said the children.

'The gnome has got into whatever place there is at the top of the tree today,' said the biggest elf. 'He may live there for months and never come down again. It's no good waiting for him – and it's certainly no good going after him. His name is Creepy, because he is for ever creeping about quietly.'

The children looked up into the broad, leafy boughs of the tree. They felt tremendously excited. The Faraway Tree in the Enchanted Wood! Oh, what magic there seemed to be in the very names!

'If only we could climb up!' said Joe longingly.

'You must never do that,' said the elves at once. 'It's dangerous. We must go now – but we do thank you for your help. If ever you want us to help *you*, just come into the Enchanted Wood and whistle seven times under the oak tree not far from our toadstools.'

'Thank you,' said the children, and stared after the six small elves as they ran off between the trees. Joe thought it was time to go home, so they followed the little men down the narrow green path until they came to the part of the wood they knew. They picked up their basket and went home, all of them thinking the same thought:

'We *must* go up the Faraway Tree and see what is at the top!'

III. UP THE FARAWAY TREE

The children did not tell their father and mother about the happenings in the Enchanted Wood, for they were so afraid that they might be forbidden to go there. But when they were alone they talked about nothing else.

'When do you suppose we could go up the Faraway Tree?' Frannie kept asking. 'Oh, do let's go, Joe.'

Joe wanted to go very badly – but he was a little afraid of what might happen, and he knew that he ought to look after his two sisters and see that no harm came to them. Just suppose they all went up the Faraway Tree and never came back!

Then he had an idea. 'Listen,' he said. 'I know what we'll do. We'll climb up the tree and just *see* what is at the top! We don't need to go there – we can just look. We'll wait until we have a whole day to ourselves, then we'll go.'

The girls were so excited. They worked hard in the house hoping that their mother would say they could have the whole day to themselves. Joe worked hard in the garden, too, clearing away all the weeds. Their parents were very pleased.

'Would you like to go to the nearest town and have a day there?' asked Mother, at last.

'No, thank you,' said Joe, at once. 'We've had enough of towns, Mother! What we'd really like is to

13

go and have a whole-day picnic in the wood!'

'Very well,' said Mother. 'You can go tomorrow. Father is going off for the day to buy some things we need. And I have things to do here in the cottage. So, as I'll be close by you can take your lunch and dinner and go off by yourselves, if it is fine and sunny.'

How the children hoped the day would be fine! They woke early and jumped out of bed. They pulled their curtains open and looked out. The sky was as blue as cornflowers. The sun shone between the trees, and the shadows lay long and dewy on the grass. The Enchanted Wood stood dark and mysterious behind their garden.

They all had breakfast, then Mother cut sandwiches, and put them in a bag along with three cakes each. She sent Joe to pick some plums from the garden, and told Beth to take two bottles of lemonade. The children were most excited.

Father set off to town, and the children waved goodbye to him from the gate. Then they tore off indoors to get the bag in which their food had been put. They said goodbye to their mother and slammed the cottage door. Ah, adventures were in the air that morning!

'Up the Faraway Tree,
Joe, Beth and Me!'

sang Frannie loudly.

'Hush!' said Joe. 'We are not far from the Enchanted Wood. We don't want anyone to know what we're going to do.'

They ran down the back garden and
out of the little gate at the end. They stood
still in the overgrown, narrow lane and
looked at one another. It was the first big adventure of
their lives! What were they going to see? What were
they going to do?

They jumped over the ditch and into the wood. At
once they felt different. Magic was all around them.
The birds' songs sounded different. The trees once
again whispered secretly to one another: 'Wisha-
wisha-wisha-wisha!'

'Ooooh! said Frannie, shivering with delight.

'Come on,' said Joe, going down the green path.
'Let's find the Faraway Tree.'

They followed him. He went on until he came to
the oak tree under which they had sat before. There
were the six toadstools too, on which the elves had
held their meeting, though the toadstools looked
rather brown and old now.

'Which is the way now?' said Beth, stopping. None
of them knew. They set off down a little path, but they
soon stopped, for they came to a strange place where
the trees stood so close together that they could go no
farther. They went back to the oak tree.

'Let's go this other way,' said Beth, so they set off in
a different direction. But this time they came to a
curious pond, whose waters were pale yellow, and
shone like butter. Beth didn't like the look of the pond
at all, and the three of them went back once more to
the oak tree.

'This is too bad,' said Frannie,
almost crying. 'Just when we've

got a whole day to ourselves we can't find the tree!'

'I'll tell you what we'll do,' said Joe suddenly. 'We'll call those elves. Don't you remember how they said they would help us whenever we wanted them?'

'Of course!' said Frannie. 'We had to stand under this oak tree and whistle seven times!'

'Go on, Joe, whistle,' said Beth. So Joe stood beneath the thick green leaves of the old oak and whistled loudly, seven times – 'Phooee, phooee, phooee, phooee, phooee, phooee, phooee!'

The children waited. In about half a minute a rabbit popped its head out of a nearby rabbit-hole and stared at them.

'Who do you want?' said the rabbit, in a furry sort of voice.

The children stared in surprise. They had never heard an animal speak before. The rabbit put his ears up and down and spoke again, rather crossly.

'Are you deaf? Who do you WANT? I said.'

'We want one of the elves,' said Joe, finding his tongue at last.

The rabbit turned and called down his hole, 'Mr Whiskers! Mr Whiskers! There's someone wanting you!'

There came a voice shouting something in answer, and then one of the six elves squeezed out of the rabbit-hole and stared at the children.

'Sorry to be so long,' he said. 'One of the rabbit's children has the measles, and I was down seeing to it.'

'I didn't think rabbits got the measles,' said Beth, astonished.

'They more often get the weasels,' said Mr

Whiskers. 'Weasels are even more catching than measles, as far as rabbits are concerned!'

He grinned as if he had made a huge joke, but as the children had no idea that weasels were savage little animals that caught rabbits, they didn't laugh.

'We wanted to ask you the way to the Faraway Tree,' said Beth. 'We've forgotten it.'

'I'll take you,' said Mr Whiskers, whose name was really a very good one, for his beard reached his toes. Sometimes he trod on it, and this jerked his head downwards suddenly. Beth kept wanting to laugh but she thought she had better not. She wondered why he didn't tie it round his waist out of the way of his feet.

Mr Whiskers led the way between the dark trees. At last he reached the trunk of the enormous Faraway Tree. 'Here you are!' he said. 'Are you expecting someone down it today?'

'Well, no,' said Joe. 'We rather wanted to go up it by ourselves.'

'Go up it by yourselves!' said Mr Whiskers, in horror. 'Don't be silly. It's dangerous. You don't know what might be at the top. There's a different place almost every day!'

'Well, we're going,' said Joe firmly, and he set his foot against the trunk of the tremendous tree and took hold of a branch above his head. 'Come on, girls!'

'I shall fetch my brothers and get you down,' said Mr Whiskers, in a fright, and he scuttled off, crying. 'It's so dangerous! It's so dangerous!'

'Do you suppose it *is* all right to go?' asked Beth, who was usually the sensible one.

'Come on, Beth!' said Joe impatiently. 'We're only

going to *see* what's at the top! Don't be a baby!'

'I'm not,' said Beth, and she and Frannie hauled themselves up beside Joe. 'It doesn't look *very* difficult to climb. We'll soon be at the top.'

But it wasn't as easy as they thought, as you will see!

IV. THE FOLK IN THE FARAWAY TREE

Before very long the children were hidden in the branches as they climbed upwards. When Mr Whiskers came back with five other elves, not a child could be seen!

'Hey, come down!' yelled the elves, dancing round the tree. 'You'll be captured or lost. This tree is dangerous!'

Joe laughed and peered down. The Faraway Tree seemed to be growing acorns just where he was, so he picked one and threw it down. It hit Mr Whiskers on the hat and he rushed away, shouting, 'Oh, something's hit me! Something's hit me!'

Then there was silence. 'They've gone,' said Joe, laughing again. 'I expect they don't much like when it rains acorns, funny little things! Come on, girls!'

'This must be an oak tree if it grows acorns,' said Beth, as she climbed. But just as she said that she stared in surprise at something nearby. It was a prickly chestnut case, with hard nuts inside!

'Good gracious!' she said. 'It's growing horse chestnuts just here! What a very peculiar tree!'

'Well, let's hope it will grow apples and pears higher up,' said Frannie, with a giggle. 'It's a most extraordinary tree!'

Soon they were quite high up. When Joe parted the leaves and tried to see out of the tree he was amazed to find that he was far higher than the tallest tree in the wood. He and the girls looked down on the top of all the other trees, which looked like a broad green carpet below.

Joe was higher up than the girls. Suddenly he gave a shout. 'I say, girls! Come up here by me, quickly! I've found something odd!'

Beth and Frannie climbed quickly up.

'Why, it's a window in the tree!' said Beth, in astonishment. They all peered inside, and suddenly the window was flung open and an angry little face looked out, with a nightcap on.

'Rude creatures!' shouted the angry little man, who looked like a pixie. 'Everybody that climbs the tree peeps in at me! It doesn't matter what I'm doing, there's always someone peeping!'

The children were too astonished to do anything but stare. The pixie disappeared and came back with a jug of water. He flung it at Beth and soaked her. She gave a scream.

'Perhaps you won't peep into other people's houses next time,' said the pixie with a grin, and he slammed his window shut again and drew the curtain.

'Well!' said Beth, trying to wipe herself dry with her handkerchief. 'What a rude little man!'

'We'd better not look in at any windows we pass,' said Joe. 'But I was so surprised to *see* a window in the tree!'

Beth soon got dry. They climbed up again, and soon had another surprise. They came to a broad branch that led to a yellow door set neatly in the big trunk of the Faraway Tree. It had a little door-knocker and a brightly-polished bell. The children stared at the door.

'I wonder who lives there?' said Frannie.

'Shall we knock and see?' said Joe.

'Well, I don't want water all over me again,' said Beth.

'We'll ring the bell and then hide behind this branch,' said Joe. 'If anyone thinks he is going to throw water at us he won't find us.'

So Joe rang the bell and then they all hid carefully behind a big branch. A voice came from the inside of the door.

'I'm washing my hair! If that's the butcher, please leave a pound of sausages!'

The children stared at one another and laughed. It was odd to hear of butchers coming up the Faraway Tree. The voice shouted again:

'If it's the oil man, I don't want anything. If it's the red dragon, he must call again next week!'

'Good gracious!' said Beth, looking rather frightened. 'The red dragon! I don't like the sound of that!'

At that moment the yellow door opened and a small fairy looked out. Her hair was fluffed out round her shoulders, drying, and she was rubbing it with a towel. She stared at the peeping children.

'Did *you* ring my bell?' she asked. 'What do you want?'

'We just wanted to see who lived in the funny little tree-house,' said Joe, peering in at the dark room inside the tree. The fairy smiled. She had a very sweet face.

'Come in for a moment,' she said. 'My name is Silky, because of my silky hair. Where are you off to?'

'We are climbing the Faraway Tree to see what is at the top,' said Joe.

'Be careful you don't find something horrid,' said Silky, giving them each a chair in her dark little tree-room. 'Sometimes there are delightful places at the top of the tree – but sometimes there are strange lands too. Last week there was the land of Hippety-Hop, which was dreadful. As soon as you got there, you had to hop on one leg, and everything went hippety-hop, even the trees. Nothing ever kept still. It was most tiring.'

'It does sound exciting,' said Beth. 'Where's our food, Joe? Let's ask Silky to have some.'

Silky was pleased. She sat there brushing her beautiful golden hair and ate sandwiches with them. She brought out a tin of Pop Cakes, which were lovely. As soon as you bit into them they went pop! and you suddenly found your mouth filled with new honey from the middle of the little cakes. Frannie took seven, one after another, for she was rather greedy. Beth stopped her.

'*You'll* go pop if you eat any more!' she said.

'Do a lot of people live in this tree?' asked Joe.

'Yes, lots,' said Silky. 'They move in and out, you know. But I'm always here, and so is the Angry Pixie, down below.'

'Yes, we've seen *him*!' said Beth. 'Who else is there?'

'There's a Mister Watzisname above me,' said Silky. 'Nobody knows his name, and he doesn't know it himself, so he's called Mister Watzisname. Don't wake him if he's asleep. He might chase you. Then there's Dame Washalot. She's always washing, and as she pours her water away down the tree, you've got to look out for waterfalls!'

'This is such an interesting and exciting tree,' said Beth, finishing her cake. 'Joe, I think we ought to go now, or we'll never get to the top. Goodbye, Silky. We'll come and see you again one day.'

'Do,' said Silky. 'I'd like to be friends.'

They all left the dear little round room in the tree and began to climb once more. Not long after they heard a peculiar noise. It sounded like an aeroplane throbbing and roaring.

'But there can't be an aeroplane in this tree!' said Joe. He peered all round – and then he saw what was making the noise. A funny old gnome sat in a deckchair on a broad branch, his mouth wide open, his eyes fast shut – snoring hard!

'It's Mister Watzisname!' said Beth. 'What a noise he makes! Mind we don't wake him!'

'Shall I put a cherry in his mouth and see what happens?' asked Joe, who was always ready for a bit of mischief. The Faraway Tree was now growing cherries all around for a change, and there were plenty to pick.

'No, Joe, no!' said Beth. 'You know what Silky said – he might chase us. *I* don't want to fall out of the Faraway Tree and bump down from bough to bough, if *you* do!'

So they all crept past old Mister Watzisname, and went on climbing up and up. For a long time nothing happened except that the wind blew in the tree. The children did not pass any more houses or windows in the tree – and then they heard another noise – rather a peculiar one.

They listened. It sounded like a waterfall – and suddenly Joe guessed what it was.

'It's Dame Washalot throwing out her dirty water!' he yelled. 'Look out, Beth! Look out, Frannie!'

Down the trunk of the tree poured a lot of blue, soapy water. Joe dodged it. Frannie slipped under a broad branch. But poor old Beth got splashed from head to foot. How she shouted!

Joe and Frannie had to lend her their handkerchiefs. 'I'm so unlucky!' sighed Beth. 'That's twice I've been soaked today.'

Up they went again, passing more little doors and windows, but seeing no one else – and at last they saw above them a vast white cloud.

'Look!' said Joe, in amazement. 'This cloud has a hole in it – and the branches go up – and I believe we're at the very top of the tree! Shall we creep through the cloud-hole and see what land is above?'

'Let's!' cried Beth and Frannie – so up they went.

V. THE ROUNDABOUT LAND

One big broad branch slanted upwards at the top of the Faraway Tree. Joe climbed on to it and looked down – but he could see nothing, for a white mist swirled around and about. Above him the enormous thick white cloud stretched, with a purple hole in it through which the topmost branch of the Faraway Tree disappeared.

The children felt tremendously excited. At last they were at the very top. Joe carefully pulled himself up the final branch. He disappeared into the purple hole. Beth and Frannie followed him.

The branch came to an end and a little ladder ran through the cloud. Up the children went – and before they knew what had happened, they were out in the sunshine, in a new and very strange land.

They stood on green grass. Above them was a blue sky. A tune was playing somewhere, going on and on and on.

'It's the sort of tune a carousel or a roundabout plays, Joe,' said Beth. 'Isn't it?'

It was – and then, suddenly, without any warning at all, the whole land began to swing round! The children almost fell over, with the swing-round beginning so suddenly.

'What's happening?' said Beth, frightened. The children felt terribly dizzy, for trees, distant houses, hills, and bushes began to move round. They too felt themselves moving, for the grass was going round as well. They looked for the hole in the cloud – but it had disappeared.

'The whole land is going round and round like a roundabout!' cried Joe, shutting his eyes with dizziness. 'We've passed over the hole in the clouds – we don't know where the topmost branch of the Faraway Tree is now – it's somewhere beneath this land, but goodness knows where!'

'Joe! But how can we get back home again?' cried Frannie, in a fright.

'We'll have to ask someone for help,' said Joe.

The three began to walk away from the patch of green field in which they were standing. Beth noticed that they had been standing on a ring of grass that seemed darker than the grass around. She wondered why it was. But she had no time to say anything, for really it was dreadfully difficult to walk properly in a land that was going round and round like a proper carousel all the time!

The music went on and on too, hurdy-gurdy, hurdy-gurdy. Joe wondered where it came from, and where the machinery was that worked the strange Roundabout Land.

Soon they met a tall man singing loudly from a book. Joe stopped him, but he went on singing. It was annoying.

'Hey-diddle, ho-diddle, round and round and round!' shouted the man, whilst Joe tried to make himself heard.

'How can we get away from this land?' Joe shouted.

'Don't interrupt me, hey-diddle, ho-diddle!' sang the man, and he beat time with his finger. Joe caught hold of the bony finger and shouted again.

'Which is the way out of this land, and what land is it?'

'Now you've made me lose my time,' said the tall man crossly. 'I shall have to begin my song again.'

'What is this land, please?' asked Frannie.

'It's Roundabout Land,' said the tall man. 'I should have thought anyone would have guessed that. You can't get away from it. It goes round and round always, and only stops once in a blue moon.'

'There must have been a blue moon when *we* climbed into it!' groaned Joe. 'It had certainly stopped then.'

The man went off, singing loudly. 'Hey-diddle, ho-diddle, round and round and round.'

'Silly old round-and-round!' said Frannie. 'Really, we do seem to meet the most peculiar people!'

'What I'm worried about is getting home,' said Beth. 'Mother will be anxious if we are not back before long. What shall we do, Joe?'

'Let's sit down under this tree and have a bit more to eat,' said Joe. So they sat down, and munched solemnly, hearing roundabout music going on all the time, and watching the distant hills and trees swinging round against the sky. It was all very strange.

Presently a pair of rabbits lolloped up and looked at the children. Frannie loved animals and she threw a bit of cake to them. To her surprise one of the rabbits picked up the cake in its paw and nibbled it like a monkey!

'Thanks!' said the rabbit. 'It's a change from grass! Where do you come from? We haven't seen you before, and we thought we knew everyone here. Nobody new ever comes to Roundabout Land.'

'And nobody ever gets away,' said the other rabbit, smiling at Frannie, and holding out its paw for a bit of cake too.

'Really?' said Beth, in alarm. 'Well, we are new to it, for we only came about an hour ago. We came up the Faraway Tree.'

'What!' cried both rabbits at once, flopping up their long ears in amazement. 'Up the *Faraway* Tree, did you say? Goodness, you don't mean to say that's touching this land?'

'Yes, it is,' said Beth. 'But I expect as this land is swinging round and round, that the topmost branch might be almost anywhere underneath it – there's no way of finding out.'

'Oh yes, there is!' said the first rabbit excitedly. 'If we burrow down a little way, and make a hole, we can see whereabouts the Faraway Tree is underneath, and we can wait for it to come round again, when the Land swings above it.'

'Well, we came up from the tree just where the grass was darker than the rest,' said Beth. 'I noticed that. Do you suppose that as the Roundabout Land swings round, it will come back to the same place again, and we could slip down the topmost branch?'

'Of course!' said the rabbits. 'We can easily burrow down that green patch of grass, and wait for the Land to turn around just over the tree again. Come on, quickly, there's no time to lose!'

All of them jumped up and sped off. Beth knew the way and so did the rabbits. Soon they were back in the field where the ring of dark grass stood. There was no opening now, leading through a cloud down to the tree. It had gone.

The rabbits began to dig quickly. Soon they found the ladder that led upwards. Then they made such a big hole that the children could see down it to a large white cloud that swirled below the Roundabout Land.

'Nothing there yet,' said the first rabbit, getting out a handkerchief and wiping his dirty front paws. 'We must wait a bit. I only hope the Land hasn't swung on and passed the Faraway Tree altogether!'

The roundabout music went on and on, then suddenly it began to slow down. One of the rabbits peeped out of the hole below and gave a shout.

'The Land has stopped going round – and the Faraway Tree is just nearby – but we can't reach it!'

The children peered through the cloud below the ladder and saw quite clearly that the Faraway Tree was very near – but not near enough to jump on. Whatever were they to do?

'Now don't try to jump,' warned the rabbits, 'or you'll fall right through the cloud.'

'But what shall we *do*?' asked Beth, in despair. 'We *must* get on the tree before we swing away again!'

'I've got a rope,' said one of the rabbits suddenly, and he put his hand into a big pocket and pulled out a yellow rope. He made a loop in one end and then threw it carefully at the topmost branch of a nearby tree. It caught and held! Good!

'Frannie, slip down the rope first,' said Joe. 'I'll hold this end.'

So Frannie, rather afraid, slid down the yellow rope to the tree – and then, just as she got there, the Roundabout music began to play very loudly and quickly, and the Roundabout Land began to move!

'Quick! Quick!' shouted Frannie, as the land swung nearer to the Faraway Tree. 'Jump! Jump!'

They jumped – and the rabbits jumped after them. The Roundabout Land swung off. The big white cloud covered everything. The children and the rabbits clung to the topmost branch and looked at one another.

'We look like monkeys on a stick,' said Joe, and they all began to giggle. 'My goodness, what an adventure! I vote we don't come up here again.'

But, as you may guess, they did!

VI. MOON-FACE AND THE SLIPPERY-SLIP

The children clung to the top branches of the Faraway Tree, whilst the rabbits slid down a bit lower. They could still hear the enchanting music of the Roundabout Land as it swung round overhead.

'We'd better get home,' said Joe, in rather a quiet voice. 'It's been just a bit too exciting.'

'Come on then,' said Beth, beginning to climb down. 'It will be easier to get down than it was to climb up!'

But Frannie was very tired. She began to cry as she clung to her branch. She was the youngest, and not so strong as Joe and Beth.

'I shall fall,' she wept. 'I know I shall fall.'

Joe and Beth looked at one another in alarm. This would never do. There was such a long way to fall!

'Dear Frannie, you simply *must* try!' said Joe, gently. 'We've got to get home safely.'

But Frannie clung to her branch and wept great tears. The two rabbits looked at her, most upset. One put his paw into her hand. 'I'll help you,' he said.

But Frannie wouldn't be helped. She was tired out and afraid of everything now. She wept so loudly that two birds nearly flew off in fright.

Just as the others were really in despair, a small door flew open in the trunk of the tree not far below, and a round moon-like face looked out.

31

'Hey there! What's the matter?' shouted the moon-faced person. 'A fellow can't get any sleep at all with that awful noise going on!'

Frannie stopped crying and looked at Moon-Face in surprise. 'I'm crying because I'm frightened of climbing down the tree,' she said. 'I'm sorry I woke you up.'

Moon-Face beamed at her. 'Have you got any toffee?' he asked. (He liked chewy sweet things to eat.)

'Toffee!' said everyone in surprise. 'What do you want toffee for?'

'To eat, of course,' said Moon-Face. 'I just thought if you had any toffee to give me I'd let you slide down my slippery-slip – you get down to the bottom very quickly that way, you know.'

'A slide all the way down the Faraway Tree!' cried Joe, hardly believing his ears. 'Good gracious! Who ever would have thought of that!'

'*I* thought of it!' said Moon-Face, beaming again just like a full moon. 'I let people use it if they pay me toffee.'

'Oh!' said the three children, and looked at one another in dismay, for none of them had any toffee. Then Joe shook his head.

'We've no toffee,' he said. 'But I've a bar of chocolate, a bit squishy, but quite nice.'

'Won't do,' said Moon-Face. 'I don't like chocolate. What about the rabbits? Haven't they got any toffee either?'

The rabbits turned out their pockets. They had a very curious collection of things, but no toffee.

'Sorry,' said Moon-Face, and slammed his door

shut. Frannie began to cry again.

Joe climbed down to the door and banged on it. 'Hey, old Moon-Face!' he shouted. 'I'll bring you some lovely home-made toffee next time I'm up the tree if you'll let us use your slippery-slip.'

The door flew open again, and Moon-Face beamed out. 'Why didn't you say so before?' he asked. 'Come in.'

One by one the rabbits and the children climbed down to the door and went in. Moon-Face's house in the tree was very peculiar. It was one round room, and in the middle of it was the beginning of the slippery-slip that ran down the whole trunk of the tree, winding round and round like a spiral staircase.

Round the top of the slide was a curved bed, a curved table, and two curved chairs, made to fit the roundness of the tree-trunk. The children were astonished, and wished they had time to stay for a while. But Moon-Face pushed them towards the slide.

'You want a cushion each,' he said. 'Hey you, rabbit, take the top one and go first.'

One of the rabbits took an orange cushion and set it at the top of the slide. He sat down on it, looking a little nervous. 'Go on, hurry up!' said Moon-Face. 'You don't want to stay all night, do you?' He gave the rabbit a hard push, and the rabbit slid down the slippery-slip at a tremendous pace, his whiskers and ears blown backwards. Joe thought it looked a lovely thing to do. He went next.

He took a blue cushion, sat on it at the top of the slide and pushed off. Down he went on his cushion, his hair streaming backwards. Round and round and round went the slippery-slip inside the enormous trunk of the old tree. It was quite dark and silent, and lasted a very long time, for the Faraway Tree was tremendously tall. Joe enjoyed every second.

When he came to the bottom his feet touched a sort of trap door in the trunk at the foot of the tree and the trap flew open. Joe shot out and landed on a big tuft of green moss which was grown there to make a soft landing-place. He sat there, out of breath – then he got up quickly, for he didn't want Beth or Frannie landing on top of him.

Beth went next. She flew down on a fat pink cushion, gasping for breath, for she went so fast. Then Frannie went on a green cushion, and then the other rabbit. One by one they shot out of the little trap door, which closed itself tightly as soon as the slider had gone through.

They all sat on the ground, getting their breath and laughing, for it really was funny to shoot down inside a tree on a cushion.

The rabbits stood up first. 'We'd better be going,' they said. 'So pleased to have met you!'

They disappeared down the nearest burrow, and the children waved goodbye. Then Joe stood up.

'Come on,' he said, 'we really must get home. Goodness knows what the time is!'

'Oh, what a lovely way of getting down the Faraway Tree that was!' said Beth, jumping to her feet. 'It was so quick!'

'I loved it,' said Frannie. 'I'd like to climb up the tree every single day just so that I could slide down that super slippery-slip. But – what do we do with the cushions?'

At that moment a red squirrel, dressed in an old jumper, came out of a hole in the trunk.

'Cushions, please!' he said. The children gathered them up and handed them to the squirrel one by one. They were getting quite used to hearing animals talk to them now.

'Are you going to carry all these cushions up the tree to Moon-Face?' asked Frannie, in wonder.

The squirrel laughed. 'Of course not!' he said. 'Moon-Face lets down a rope for them. Look – here it comes!'

A rope came slipping down between the branches. The squirrel caught the end of it and tied the bundle of cushions firmly on to the rope. He gave three tugs, and the rope swung upwards again, taking the cushions with it.

'Good idea!' said Joe, and then they all turned to go home, thinking, as they walked, of the strange and exciting things that had happened that day.

They came to the ditch and jumped across. They went down the little lane and through their little back gate. By the time they reached the cottage they were ready to drop with tiredness. Their mother was still busy in the garden, and their father was not yet home.

So, sleepily, Beth made them all some hot milk, which they took up to their rooms to drink while sitting in bed.

'I'm not going up the Faraway Tree again,' said

Frannie, lying down.

'Well, *I* am!' said Joe. 'Don't forget we promised old Moon-Face some home-made toffee! We can climb up to his house, give him the toffee, and slide down that slippery-slip again. We don't need to go into any land at the top of the tree.'

But Beth and Frannie were fast asleep. And very soon Joe was too – dreaming of the strange Faraway Tree, and the curious folk who lived in its enormous trunk!

VII. BETH MAKES SOME TOFFEE FOR MOON-FACE

The children talked about nothing else but the Faraway Tree and its strange folk for days after their adventure. Beth said they must certainly keep their promise to take toffee to Moon-Face.

'Promises must never be broken,' she said. 'I will make some toffee if Mother will let me have the sugar, syrup and milk. Then when it's done you can take it to Moon-Face, Joe.'

Mother said they could make toffee on Wednesday, after she had been to the shops. So on Wednesday Beth set to work making the best, sweetest, chewiest toffee she could.

She set it in a pan on the stove. It cooked beautifully. When it had cooled and was set nice and hard, Beth broke it up into small pieces. She put them into a paper bag, gave one piece each to the others, and popped one into her own mouth.

'I'll have to go at night, I think,' said Joe. 'I shan't get any time off this week, I know. We're so busy with the garden now.'

So that night, when the moon was shining brightly in the sky overhead, Joe slipped out of bed. Beth and Frannie woke up and heard him. They hadn't meant to go with him, but when they saw the moonlight shining everywhere and thought of that exciting Faraway Tree, they felt that they simply *couldn't* stay behind! Wouldn't you have felt that too?

They dressed quickly and whispered through Joe's door. 'We're coming too, Joe. Wait for us!'

Joe waited. Then they all three slipped down the creaky stairs and out into the moonlit garden. The shadows were very black indeed, just like ink. There was no colour anywhere, only just the pale, cold moonlight.

They were soon in the Enchanted Wood. But, dear me, it was quite, quite different now! It was simply alive with people and animals! In the very dark parts of the wood little lanterns were hung in rows. In the moonlit parts there were no lanterns, and a great deal of chattering was going on.

Nobody took any notice of the children at all. Nobody seemed surprised to see them. But the children were most astonished at everything!

'There's a market over there!' whispered Joe to Beth. 'Look! There are necklaces made of painted acorns and brooches made of wild roses!'

But Beth was looking at something else – a dance going on in the moonlit dell, with fairies and pixies chattering and laughing together. Sometimes, when they were tired of dancing on their feet, partners would fly in the air and dance there in the moonlight.

Frannie was watching some elves growing toadstools. As fast as the toadstool grew, an elf laid a cloth on it and put glasses of lemonade and tiny cakes there. It was all like a strange dream.

'Oh, I *am* glad we came!' said Beth, in delight. 'Who would have thought that the Enchanted Wood would be like this at night?'

They wasted a great deal of time looking at everything, but at last they got to the Faraway Tree. And even here there was a great difference! The whole tree was hung with strings of tiny lights and glittered softly from branch to branch, rather like a very enormous Christmas Tree.

Joe saw something else. It was a stout rope going from branch to branch, for people to hold on to when they wished to go up the tree.

'Look at that!' he said. 'It will be much easier to go up tonight. All we'll have to do is just to hold on to the rope and pull ourselves up by it! Come on!'

Other folk, and some animals too, were going up the tree. Not to the land at the top, but to visit their friends who lived in the trunk of the enormous old tree. All the doors and windows were open now, and there was a great deal of laughing and talking going on.

The children climbed up and up. When they came to the window of the pixie who had been so angry with them last week because they had peeped in, they found that he was in a very good temper now, sitting smiling at his open window, talking to three owls. But Joe didn't think they had better stop, in case the pixie remembered them and threw water over them again.

So on they went holding on to the thick rope, climbing very easily. They came to Silky's house, and called her. She was at her stove, baking something.

'Hallo!' she said, looking up and smiling.

'So here you are again – just in time, too, because I'm baking Pop Cakes, and they are most delicious hot!'

Her silky golden hair stood out round her tiny face, which was red with baking. Joe took out his bag of toffee.

'We're really taking them to Moon-Face,' he said, 'but do have one!'

Silky took one and then gave them three hot Pop Cakes each. My goodness, how lovely they were, especially when they went pop in the children's mouths!

'We mustn't stop, Silky dear,' said Beth. 'We've still a long way to go up the tree.'

'Well, look out for Dame Washalot's washing water, then,' said Silky. 'She's dreadful at night. She knows there are a lot of people up and down the tree, and she just loves to soak them with her dirty water!'

The children went on up. They passed Mister Watzisname, still fast asleep and snoring in his chair, and dodged Dame Washalot's water sloshing down. Nobody even got splashed this time! Frannie laughed.

'This really is the funniest tree I ever knew,' she said. 'You simply never know what's going to happen!'

They pulled themselves up and up by the rope and came at last to the top. They knocked on Moon-Face's yellow door. 'Come in!' yelled a voice, and in they went.

Moon-Face was sitting on his curved bed, mending one of his cushions. 'Hallo!' he said. 'Did you bring me that toffee you owe me?'

'Yes,' said Joe, handing him the bag. 'There's a lot there, Moon-Face – half to pay you for last week's slippery-slide, and half to pay you if you'll let us go down again tonight.'

'Oh my!' said Moon-Face, looking with great delight into the bag. 'What lovely toffee!'

He crammed four large pieces into his mouth and sucked with joy.

'Is it nice?' said Beth.

'Ooble-ooble-ooble-ooble!' answered Moon-Face, quite unable to speak properly, for his teeth were all stuck together with the toffee! The children laughed.

'Is the Roundabout Land at the top of the Faraway Tree?' asked Joe.

Moon-Face shook his head. 'Oooble!' he said.

'What land is there now?' asked Frannie.

Moon-Face made a face, and screwed up his nose. 'Oooble-oooble-oooble-oooble-oooble!' he said very earnestly.

'Oh dear, we shan't be able to get anything out of him at all whilst he's eating toffee,' said Beth. 'He'll just ooble away. What a pity! I *would* have liked to know what strange land was there tonight.'

'I'll just go and peep!' said Joe, jumping up. Moon-Face looked alarmed. He shook his head, and caught hold of Joe. 'Oooble-oooble-oooble-oooble!' he cried.

'It's all right, Moon-Face, I'm only going to peep,' said Joe. 'I shan't go into the land.'

'OOBLE-OOBLE-OOBLE-OOBLE!' cried Moon-Face in a fright, trying his best to swallow all the toffee so that he could speak properly. 'Oooble!'

Joe didn't listen. He went out of the door with the girls, and climbed up the last branch of the Faraway Tree. What strange land was above it this time? Joe peered up through the dark hole in the cloud, through which a beam of moonlight shone down.

He came to the little ladder that ran up the hole in the cloud. He climbed up it. His head poked out into the land at the top. He gave a shout.

'Beth! Frannie! It's a kind of ice and snow! There are big white bears everywhere! Oh, do come and look!'

But then a dreadful thing happened! Something lifted Joe right off the ladder – and he disappeared into the land of ice and snow above the cloud.

'Come back! Joe, come back!' yelled Moon-Face, swallowing all his toffee in fright. 'You mustn't even look, or the Snowman will get you!'

But Joe was gone. Beth looked at Moon-Face in dismay. 'What *shall* we do?' she said.

VIII. JOE AND THE MAGIC SNOWMAN

Moon-Face was most upset to see Joe disappear. 'I told him not to – I told him!' he groaned.

'You didn't,' sobbed Frannie. 'Your mouth was full of toffee and all you could say was 'Oooble-oobleooble!' And how could we know what that meant?'

'Where's Joe now?' asked Beth, quite pale with shock.

Yes, indeed – where *was* Joe? Someone had lifted him right off the ladder, up into the Land of Ice and Snow! And there, strangely enough, the moon and the sun were in the sky at the same time, one at one side and the other opposite, both shining with a pale light.

Joe shivered, for it was very cold. He looked up to see what had lifted him off the ladder, and he saw in front of him a big strange creature – a snowman! He was just like the snowmen Joe had so often made in the wintertime – round and fat and white, with an old hat stuck on his head and a carrot for a nose.

'This is luck!' said the Snowman, in a soft, snowy sort of voice. 'I've been standing by that hole for days, waiting for a seal to come up – and *you* came!'

'Oh,' said Joe, remembering that seals came up to breathe through holes in the ice. 'That wasn't a waterhole – that was the hole that led down the Faraway Tree. I want to go back, please.'

'The hole has closed up,' said the Snowman. Joe

looked – and to his great dismay he saw that a thick layer of ice had formed over the hole – so thick that he knew perfectly well he could never break through it.

'Whatever shall I do now?' he said.

'Just what I tell you,' said the Snowman, with a grin. 'This is splendid! In this dull and silent land there is nothing but polar bears and seals and penguins. I have often wanted someone to talk to.'

'How did you get here?' asked Joe, wrapping his coat firmly round him, for he was bitterly cold.

'Ah,' said the Snowman, 'that's a long story! I was made by some children long ago – and when they had finished me, they laughed at me and threw stones at me to break me up. So that night I crept away here – and made myself King, but what's the good of being King if you've only bears and things to talk to? What I want is a really good servant who can talk my language. And now *you've* come!'

'But I don't want to be your servant,' said Joe indignantly.

'Nonsense!' said the Snowman, and he gave Joe a push that nearly sent him over. Then, on big, flat snow-feet he moved forward to where there was a low wall of snow.

'Make me a good house,' he said.

'I don't know how to!' said Joe.

'Oh, just cut blocks of this stiff icy snow and build them up one on top of another,' said the Snowman. 'When you've finished I'll give you a warm coat to wear. Then you won't shiver so much.'

Joe didn't see that he could do anything but obey. So he picked up a shovel that was lying by the wall

44

and began to cut big bricks of the frozen snow. When he had cut about twenty he stopped and placed them one on top of another till one side of the round house was made. Then he began to cut snow-bricks again, wondering all the time how in the world he would ever be able to escape from this strange land.

Joe had often built little snow-houses of soft snow in his garden at home during the winter. Now had made a big one, with proper snow-blocks, as hard as bricks. He quite enjoyed it, though he did wish the girls were there too. When he had finished it, and made a nice rounded roof, the Snowman came shuffling up.

'Very nice,' he said, 'very nice indeed. I can just get in, I think.'

He squeezed his big snow-body inside, and threw out a thick coat for Joe, made of wool as soft and as white as the snow all around. Joe put it on very thankfully. Then he tried to squeeze in after the Snowman, for he wanted to be out of the cold, icy wind.

But he was so squashed between the Snowman and the walls of the snow-house that he couldn't breathe.

'Don't push so,' said the Snowman disagreeably. 'Move up.'

'I can't!' gasped poor Joe. He felt quite certain that he would be pushed right out of the snow-hut through a hole in the wall!

Just then there came a curious grunt at the doorway. The Snowman called out at once.

'Is that you, Furry? Take this boy to your home under the ice. He's a nuisance here. He keeps squashing me!'

Joe looked up to see who Furry was – and he saw a great white bear looking in. The bear had a stupid but kind look on his face.

'Ooomph!' said the bear, and pulled Joe out into the open air. Joe knew it was no use to struggle. Nobody could get away from a bear as big as that! But the bear was certainly very kindly.

'Oooomph?' he said to Joe, with a loud grunting noise.

'I don't know what you mean,' said Joe.

The bear said no more. He just took Joe along with him, half carrying the little boy, for Joe found the way very slippery indeed.

They came to a hole that led under the ice and snow. The bear pushed Joe down it – and to Joe's enormous surprise he found there was a big room underneath, with five bears there, big and little! It was quite warm there too – Joe was astonished, for there was no heater, of course.

'Ooomph,' said all the bears politely.

'Ooomph!' said Joe. That pleased the bears very much indeed. They came and shook paws with Joe very solemnly and oomphed all over him.

Joe liked the look of the bears much more than he liked the look of the Snowman. He thought perhaps they might help him to escape from this silly land of ice and snow.

'Could you tell me the way back to the Faraway Tree?' he asked the bears politely and clearly.

The bears looked at one another and then ooomphed at Joe. It was quite clear that they didn't understand a word he said.

'Never mind,' said Joe, with a sigh, and made up his mind to put up with things till he could see a way to escape.

The Snowman was a great nuisance. No sooner did Joe settle himself down for a nap, leaning his head against the big warm body of a bear, than there came a call from the snow-house.

'Hey, boy! Come here and play dominoes with me!'

So Joe had to go and play dominoes, and as the Snowman wouldn't let him come into the house because he said he was squashed, Joe had to sit at the doorway and play, and he nearly froze to bits.

Then another time, just as he was eating a nice bit of fried fish that one of the bears had kindly cooked for him, the Snowman shouted to him to come and make him a window in his house. And Joe had to hurry off and cut a sheet of clear ice to fit into one side of the snow-house for a window! Really, that Snowman was a perfect nuisance!

I wish to goodness I'd never stepped into this silly land, thought Joe a hundred times. It's a good thing the bears are so nice to me. I only wish they could say something else besides 'Ooomph.'

Joe wondered what Beth and Frannie were doing. Were they very upset when he didn't come back? Would they go home and tell their father and mother what had happened?

Beth and Frannie *were* upset! It had been dreadful to see poor Joe disappear through the cloud like that.

Moon-Face looked very solemn too. He could speak quite well now that he had swallowed all his toffee.

'We must rescue him,' he said, his face shining like the full moon.

'How?' asked the girls.

'I must think,' said Moon-Face, and he shut his eyes. His head swelled up with his thinking. He opened his eyes and nodded his head.

'We'll go to Goldilocks and the Three Bears,' he said. 'Her bears know the Land of Ice and Snow. She might be able to help Joe that way.'

'But where does Goldilocks live?' asked Beth, in wonder. 'I thought she was just a fairy tale.'

'Good gracious, no!' said Moon-Face. 'Come on – we'll have to catch the train.'

'What train?' asked Frannie, in astonishment.

'Oh, wait and see!' said Moon-Face. 'Hurry now – go down the slippery-slip and wait for me at the bottom!'

IX. THE HOUSE OF THE
THREE BEARS

Beth took a cushion, put it at the top of the slide, and pushed off. Down she went, whizzzzzzz! She shot to the bottom, flew out of the trap door and landed on the cushion of moss. She had hardly got up before Frannie flew out of the trap door too.

'You know, that slippery-slip is the greatest fun!' said Beth. 'I'd like to do that all day long!'

'Yes, if only we didn't have to climb all the way up the tree first,' said Frannie.

The trap door flew open and out shot Moon-Face on a yellow cushion. He put the three cushions together, whistled to the red squirrel who looked after them, and threw them to him. Then he turned to the waiting girls.

'There's a train at midnight,' he said. 'We shall have to hurry.'

The wood was still bright with moonlight. The three of them hurried between the trees. Suddenly Beth heard the chuffing of a train, and she and Frannie stopped in surprise. They saw a small train winding in and out of the trees, looking for all the world like a old-fashioned clockwork toy train made big! The engine even had a key in its side – as if to wind it up!

There was a small station nearby. Moon-Face caught hold of the girls' hands and ran to it. The train was standing quite still there.

The carriages had tin doors and windows which didn't open, just like those of a clockwork train. Beth tried her hardest to open a door, but it was no use. The train whistled. It was anxious to be off.

'Don't you know how to get into this train?' asked Moon-Face, with a laugh. 'You *are* sillies! You just slide the roof off!'

As he spoke he pushed at the roof – and it slid off like the roof of a toy train's carriage.

'I think this is just a toy clockwork train made big,' said Frannie, climbing over the side of the carriage and getting in at the roof. 'I never saw such a funny train in my life!'

They all got in. Moon-Face couldn't seem to slide the roof on again properly, so he stood up inside the carriage, and when the train went off, Beth and Frannie, who couldn't possibly see out of the tin windows, stood up and looked out of the roof instead. They did look funny!

At the next station, which was called 'Dolls' Station', three dolls got into the carriage and stared at them very hard. One was so like Beth's own doll at home that she couldn't help staring back.

The second station was called 'Crosspatch Station', and standing next to the railway tracks were three of the crossest-looking old women that the girls had ever seen. One of them got into their carriage, and the three dolls at once got out, and climbed into the next one.

'Move up!' said the Crosspatch angrily to

Moon-Face. He moved up.

The Crosspatch was an uncomfortable person to travel with. She grumbled all the time, and her basket, which was full of prickly bunches of roses, kept bumping into poor Frannie.

'Here we are, here we are!' sang out Moon-Face, when they got to the next station, and the three of them got out gladly, leaving the Crosspatch grumbling away all to herself.

The station was called 'Bears Station', and there were a great many teddy-bears about, some brown, some pink, some blue, and some white. When they wanted to talk to one another they kept pressing themselves in the middle, where the button that made them talk was, and then they could talk quite well. Frannie wanted to giggle when she saw them doing this. It did look so funny.

'Please could you tell me the way to the Three Bears' House?' Moon-Face asked a blue teddy-bear politely.

The bear pressed himself in the middle and answered in a nice growly voice, 'Up the lane and down the lane and around the lane.'

'Thank you,' said Moon-Face.

'It sounds a bit funny to me,' said Beth doubtfully.

'Not at all,' said Moon-Face, leading them up a little lane through the honeysuckle. 'Here we are, going *up* a lane – and now you see it goes downhill – so we're going down – and presently we'll turn a corner and go *around* the lane!'

He was right. They went up and then down and then around – and there in front of them, tucked into a woody corner, was the dearest, prettiest little house the girls had ever seen! It was covered with pink roses from top to bottom, and its tiny windows winked in the moonlight as if they had eyes.

Moon-Face knocked at the door. A sleepy voice cried, 'Come in!' Moon-Face opened the door and they all went in. There was a table in front of them, and on it were three steaming bowls of what some people call porridge, and some call oatmeal, and round it were three chairs, one big, one middle-sized, and one tiny.

'It's the House of the Three Bears all right!' whispered Beth excitedly. It was just like seeing a fairy story come true!

'We're here!' said the voice from another room. Moon-Face went in with Beth and Frannie. The other room was a small bedroom, with a big bed in it, a middle-sized bed, and in the cot was a most adorable baby bear with the bluest eyes the girls had ever seen.

'Where's Goldilocks?' asked Moon-Face.

'Gone shopping,' said the father bear.

'Where does she sleep when she's here?' asked Beth, looking round. 'And does she always live with you now?'

'Always,' said the father bear, putting his big nightcap straight. 'She looks after us very well. There's a market on tonight in the Enchanted Wood and she's gone to see if she can buy some porridge cheap. As for where she sleeps, well, she just chooses any of our beds, you know, and we cuddle up together then. But she likes the baby bear's bed best, because it's so soft and warm.'

'She did in the story,' said Frannie.

'What story?' asked the mother bear.

'Well – the story of the three bears,' said Frannie.

'Never heard of it,' said the three bears, all together, which really seemed rather extraordinary to Beth and Frannie. They didn't like to ask any more questions after that.

'Here's Goldilocks now!' said the mother bear. The sound of a little high voice could be heard coming nearer and nearer. The baby bear sprang out of his cot and ran to the door in delight.

A pretty little girl with long, curling golden hair picked him up and hugged him. 'Hallo, dearest!' she said. 'Have you been a good bear?'

Then she saw Beth, Frannie and Moon-Face, and stared at them in surprise. 'Who are you?' she said.

Moon-Face explained about Joe, and how he had gone to the Land of Ice and Snow, where the big white bears lived.

'I'm afraid the Magic Snowman will make him a prisoner there,' said Moon-Face. 'And he'll have to live with the white bears. Could you get your three bears to come with us and ask the white bears to let Joe go free, Goldilocks?'

'But I don't know the way,' said Goldilocks.

'*We* do!' said the father bear suddenly. 'The white bears are cousins of ours. Moon-Face, if you can help us with a little bit of magic, we can visit the Land of Ice and Snow in a few minutes!'

'Good gracious!' said Beth, most astonished. 'But it's ever so far away, right at the top of the Faraway Tree!'

'That doesn't matter,' said the father bear. He took down a large jar from the mantelpiece and filled it with water. He put into it a yellow powder and stirred it with a big black crow's feather.

Moon-Face put his hands into the water and began to sing a string of such strange words that Beth and Frannie felt quite trembly. The water bubbled. It rose up to the top of the jar. It overflowed and ran on to the floor. It turned to ice beneath their feet! A cold wind filled the little house and everyone shivered.

Then Beth looked out of the window – and what she saw there filled her with such amazement that she couldn't say a word, but just pointed.

Frannie looked too – and whatever do you think? Outside lay nothing but ice and snow – they were in the same land as Joe! Though how this land happened neither Beth nor Frannie could make out.

'We're there,' said Moon-Face, taking his hands out of the jar and drying them on his red handkerchief. 'Can you lend us any coats, bears? We shall be cold here.'

The mother bear handed them thick coats out of a cupboard. They put them on. The bears already had thick fur and did not need anything extra.

'Now to go and find Joe!' said Moon-Face. 'Come on, bears – you've got to help!'

X. THE BATTLE OF THE BEARS

Goldilocks, the Three Bears, the girls, and Moon-Face all went out of the little cottage. How strange it seemed to see roses blossoming over the walls, when ice and snow lay all around!

'The thing is – *where* do we go to find the polar bears?' said Goldilocks.

'Over there, towards the sun,' said the father bear. Beth and Frannie were surprised to see both the moon and the sun shining in the sky. They followed the father bear, slipping and sliding, and holding on to one another. It was very cold, and their noses and toes felt as if they were freezing.

Suddenly they saw the little snow-house that Joe had built for the Magic Snowman.

'Look!' said the father bear. 'We'd better make for that.'

But before they got there a big white figure squeezed itself out of the snow-house and saw them. It was the Magic Snowman! As soon as he saw the Three Bears and the others, he began to shout loudly in a windy, snowy voice:

'Enemies! Enemies! Hey, bears, come and send off the enemies!'

'We're not enemies,' yelled Moon-Face, and Goldilocks ran forward to show the Snowman that she was a little girl. But Moon-Face pulled her back. He didn't trust that old Snowman!

The Snowman bent his big fat body down and picked up great handfuls of snow. He threw one at Goldilocks. She ducked down, and it passed over her and hit the baby bear.

'Oooooch!' he said, and sat down in a hurry. Then everything happened at once. A crowd of white polar bears hurried out of their underground home to help the Snowman, and soon the air was full of flying snowballs. The snow was hard, and the balls hurt when they hit anyone. It wasn't a bit of good the girls shouting that they were friends, not enemies. Nobody heard them, and soon there was a fierce battle going on!

'Oh dear!' gasped Beth, trying her best to throw straight. 'This is dreadful! We shall never rescue Joe by behaving like this!'

But there really didn't seem anything else to be done! After all, if people are fighting you, you can't do much but defend yourself, and the Three Bears, and the girls, and Moon-Face felt very angry at having hard snowballs thrown at them.

Smack! Thud! Biff! Squish! The snowballs burst as they hit, and soon there was a great noise of angry 'Ooomphs' from the white bears, and 'Oooches' from the teddy-bears, and yells from the children, and screeches from Moon-Face, who acted as if he was mad, hopping about and yelling and kicking up the snow as well as throwing it! His big round face was a fine target for snowballs, and he was hit more than anybody else. Poor Moon-Face!

Now whilst this fierce battle was going on, where do

you suppose Joe was? As soon as he heard the cry of 'Enemies! Enemies!' he had hidden in a corner, for he didn't want to be mixed up in any fight. When he saw the white bears going out, and he was left all alone, he began at once to think of escaping.

He crept to the hole that led above-ground. The battle was some way off, so Joe did not see that the enemies were really his own friends! If he had he would have gone to join them at once.

What a terrible noise they are all making! he thought. It sounds like a battle between gorillas and bears to me! I'm not going near them – I'd be eaten up or something! I shall just run hard the opposite way and hope I'll meet someone to help me.

So Joe, dressed in his big white woolly coat, and looking just like a little white bear himself, crept off over the ice and snow, not seen by anyone. He ran as soon as he thought he was out of sight. He ran and he ran and he ran.

But he met nobody. Not a soul was to be seen. Only a lonely seal lay on a shelf of ice, but even he dived below as soon as he saw Joe.

And then Joe stopped in the greatest astonishment and stared as if his eyes would fall out of his head. He had come to the cottage of the Three Bears, standing all alone in the middle of the ice and snow – and, of course, its roses were still blooming round it, scenting the air.

'I'm dreaming!' said Joe. 'I simply *must* be dreaming! A cottage – with roses – here in the middle of the snow! Well – I shall go and see who lives there.

Perhaps they would give me something to eat and let me rest, for I'm very hungry and tired.'

He knocked at the door. There was no answer. He opened the door and went in. How he stared! There was no one to be seen at all, but on the table stood three bowls of steaming porridge, one big, one middle-sized, and one small. It was rather dark, so Joe lighted a big candle on the table.

Then he sank down into the biggest chair – but it was far too big and he got up again. He sat down in the next sized chair – but that was too piled up with cushions, and he got up to sit in the smallest chair. That was just right, and Joe settled down comfortably – but alas, his weight was too much for it, and the chair broke to bits beneath him!

He looked at the delicious porridge. He tasted the porridge in the biggest bowl – it was much too hot and burnt his tongue. He tasted the next bowl – but that was far too sweet. But when he tasted the porridge in the little bowl, it was just right.

So Joe ate it all up! Then he felt so sleepy that he thought he really must rest. So he went into the bedroom and lay down on the biggest bed. But it was far too big, so he tried the middle-sized one. That was too soft and went down in the middle, so Joe lay down on the cot. And that was so small and warm and comfortable that he fell fast asleep!

All this time the snowball battle was going on. The Snowman was so big and the polar bears were so fierce that very soon the Three Bears, the children, and Moon-Face were driven backwards.

Then a snowstorm blew up, and the snow fell so

thickly that it was quite impossible to see anything. Moon-Face called out in alarm:

'Bears! Goldilocks! Beth! Frannie! Take hold of each other's hands at once and don't let go. One of us might easily be lost in the storm!'

Everyone at once took hands. The snow blew into their faces and they could see nothing. Bending forwards they began to walk carefully away from the white bears, who had stopped fighting now and were trying to find out where their enemies were.

'Don't shout or anything,' said Moon-Face. 'We don't want the white bears to hear us, in case they take us prisoners. They might not listen to the Three Bears. Move off, and we'll look for some sort of shelter till this storm is over.'

They were all very miserable. They were cold, rather frightened, and quite lost. They stumbled over the snow, keeping hold of one another's hands firmly. They went on and on, and suddenly Goldilocks shook off Moon-Face's hand and pointed in front of them.

'A light!' she said in astonishment. Everyone stopped.

'I say! I SAY! It's our cottage!' shrieked the baby bear, in surprise and delight. 'But who's inside? *Someone* must have lighted the candle!'

They all stared at the lighted window. Who was inside the cottage? Could the Magic Snowman have found it? Or the polar bears? Was it an enemy inside – or a friend?

'Wheeeeew!' blew the wind, and the snowflakes fell thickly on everyone as they stood there, wondering.

'Ooooh!' shivered Moon-Face. 'We shall get

dreadful colds standing out here in the snow. Let's go in, and find out who's there.'

So the father bear opened the door, and one by one they all trooped in, looking round the empty room, half afraid.

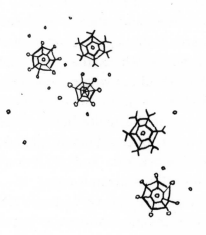

XI. MORE AND MORE SURPRISES

'There doesn't *seem* to be anyone here!' said Beth, cautiously looking around.

'Well, WHO lighted that candle?' asked Moon-Face, his big round face looking anxious. '*We* didn't leave it burning!'

Suddenly the father bear gave an angry growl, and pointed to his chair. 'Who's been sitting in *my* chair?' he said.

'And who's been sitting in *my* chair?' said the mother bear, pointing to hers.

'And who's been sitting in *my* chair and broken it all to bits?' squeaked the baby bear, in tears.

Beth giggled. 'This sounds like the story of the Three Bears coming true!' she said to Frannie. 'They'll talk about porridge next.'

They did.

'Who's been eating *my* porridge?' said the father bear angrily.

'And who's been eating *my* porridge?' said the mother bear.

'And who's been eating mine, and gobbled it all UP?' wept the baby bear, scraping his spoon round the empty plate.

'It's all very mysterious,' said Moon-Face. '*Somebody* lighted the candle – *somebody* sat in the chairs – *somebody* ate the porridge. But who?'

'Not me this time,' said Goldilocks. 'I was with you all the time we were snowballing, wasn't I, Bears?'

'You certainly were,' growled the father bear softly, patting the little girl on the back. He was very fond of her.

'I wish we had found poor Joe,' said Beth. 'Whatever will he be doing in this horrid cold land?'

'Do you suppose we ought to go out and look for him again?' said Frannie, shivering as she thought of the ice-cold wind outside.

'No,' said Moon-Face decidedly. 'No one is going out of this cottage again till we're safely in the wood at home. I'm afraid we can't possibly rescue Joe now.'

'What's that noise?' said Goldilocks suddenly. Everybody listened. *Someone* was snoring softly in the next room!

'We never thought of looking there,' said Moon-Face. 'Who can it be?'

'Shh!' said Goldilocks. 'If we can catch him asleep, we can hold him tight and he won't be able to get away. But if he wakes up he might be fierce.'

They tiptoed to the door of the bedroom. One by one they squeezed through.

'Who's been lying on *my* bed?' said the father bear, in a growly voice.

'Shh!' said Moon-Face crossly.

'Who's been lying on *my* bed?' said the mother bear.

'Shh!' said everyone.

'And who's been lying on *my* bed and is fast asleep there still?' said the baby bear.

Everyone stared at the cot. Yes – there was someone

there – someone covered in white. Was it a polar bear?

'It's a white bear!' said Moon-Face, half frightened.

'Let's lock him in before he wakes,' said the father bear. 'He might still think we are enemies!'

They all rushed out of the little room and slammed the door shut with a loud bang, locking it behind them.

'He's caught!' said Moon-Face joyfully.

Joe awoke with a jump. Who had locked him in? Had the Magic Snowman caught him again? He began to shout and bang on the door. And then Beth and Frannie recognised his voice and yelled out loudly:

'Moon-Face! It's Joe! It's Joe! It's Joe! Oh, it's Joe!'

They rushed to the door and unlocked it, and flung their arms around Joe. The boy was too astonished to speak. He hugged his sisters.

'How did you get here?' he asked.

'How did *you* get here?' cried Beth and Frannie.

'Come into the kitchen and we'll all have some hot porridge and milk,' said Goldilocks. 'We can talk then and get warm.'

So Joe went with the others, all chattering loudly about everything. Goldilocks ladled out porridge into blue bowls, and made some hot chocolate. Soon everyone was putting sugar on porridge and drinking the hot chocolate. Joe poured some milk over his porridge and smiled joyfully at everybody.

'What an adventure this has been!' he said. 'Shall I tell my tale first, or will you tell yours?'

He told his – and then Beth told how Moon-Face had gone to the Three Bears for their help, and all about the fierce snowball battle.

'It's a pity about the battle,' said the father bear mournfully. 'The white bears are cousins of ours, and have always been friendly – now they seem to be enemies.'

'Let's hope they don't discover our cottage,' said Goldilocks, eating her hot porridge. 'Moon-Face, hadn't we better make some magic and get back to the wood?'

'Plenty of time, plenty of time,' said Moon-Face, pouring himself another cup of hot chocolate.

But, you know, there *wasn't* plenty of time. For just at that moment Goldilocks gave a scream and pointed to the window.

'Someone looked in!' she said.

'Don't be silly!' said Moon-Face.

'I'm not,' said Goldilocks. 'I tell you, *somebody* looked in! Who could it be?'

'The handle of the door is moving!' yelled Moon-Face, and he leapt to the door. In a flash he had locked it and bolted it.

The father bear got up and went to the window. He looked out into the snowstorm.

'I can't see anything,' he said; and then he growled loudly. 'Yes, I can – I can see the white bears! They have surrounded our cottage! *Now* what shall we do?'

'Well, they can't get in at the door, and they *certainly* shan't get in at the window,' said Moon-Face, looking fierce. The door shook, but it held well. Someone battered on it.

'We shan't let you in!' yelled Joe.

'If anyone tries to open the window or break it, I'll throw this kettle at him!' shouted Moon-Face, who was dancing about waving the kettle in the air.

'Moon-Face, that kettle has got hot water in it,' said Frannie. 'Do be careful. You nearly dropped some on me.'

'I'll drop it on to any bear that dares to come in here!' yelled Moon-Face, spattering the room with steaming drops.

'Oh dear!' said Beth. 'Hide behind the bed, Frannie. It seems to me that Moon-Face is almost as dangerous as the bears.' Moon-Face soon realised that they were right, and that waving a hot kettle around was a foolish and dangerous thing to do. So he put it down again, gently.

Then the father bear had an idea, and dragged the big table across the room to block the door. Things were getting exciting. Joe and the girls were frightened, but they couldn't help feeling terribly thrilled too. Whatever was going to happen next?

'Oooomph! Ooooomph!' boomed the big bears outside, but they couldn't get in at the door or window.

But they found another way! The chimney was wide and big, for the fireplace was one of the large, old-fashioned kind and needed a wide chimney. One of the bears climbed up on to the roof, followed by three more. The first one slipped into the big chimney. Down he went, whooosh! Down went another – and the third – and the fourth.

They landed with a crash on to the big hearth, and hurriedly jumped away from the flames of the fire.

'Surrender!' they cried to the startled children and bears. 'Surrender! The Magic Snowman is outside! Let him in!'

XII. WHAT HAPPENED TO THE SNOWMAN

Everyone stared at the big white bears in horror. No one had thought of the chimney. What a pity they hadn't stopped it up!

'I am going to let the Magic Snowman in,' said the first white bear.

Then the father bear spoke up, in a very sorrowful voice.

'Cousin, why are we enemies? We have always been good friends up till now.'

The four white bears looked at him and at the mother bear in sudden amazement. They rushed at them with loud ooomphy noises.

Joe thought they were going to fight the Three Bears. But no, the white bears were not going to fight – they were hugging the Three Bears as tightly as they could, and to the children's amazement tears were pouring down their furry faces!

'We didn't know it was you!' said the white bears. 'Why, cousins, we would never have fought you if only we had known you were the Three Bears we love so much!'

'There, there!' said the mother bear, wiping the tears of a white bear off her fur. 'It's all right. But for goodness' sake tell the other bears we're friends. We don't want the front door battered down.'

Moon-Face opened the door and yelled out of it,

'Bears, it's all right! This is the cottage of your cousins, the Three Bears! We're friends!'

But the white bears didn't answer or come in – instead a big white shape came up and squeezed through the door – the Magic Snowman!

A chill fell over the little room. The white bears were frightened of him, for he was their master. He shut the door and glared at everyone out of his stone eyes.

'So even my own bears have gone over to the enemy!' he said. 'Oho! What will you say if I turn you into ice and snow, everyone?'

Nobody said anything. But, to Beth's surprise, Moon-Face shut the door, and then went to the fire. He piled on three great logs and winked at Beth.

The Snowman took up a white bear by the scruff of his neck and shook him.

'So you found your voices, did you?' he said. 'Didn't I tell you that you were only to say 'Ooomph' and not speak a word to anyone? I won't have bears that talk!'

He picked up another white bear and shook him. 'So you are friends with my enemies, are you?' he said.

The room became very hot. Joe took off his coat. So did the others. Moon-Face slyly put on another log. The fire crackled and shot great flames up the chimney. Frannie wished she could take off everything, she was so hot.

Whatever does Moon-Face think he is doing, making the room so hot? she thought crossly. But just as she was about to tell him what she was thinking, he winked at her, and she said nothing. Moon-Face had some strange plan that he was carrying out.

The Snowman went on and on, grumbling and threatening. Everyone listened and said nothing. Moon-Face raked the fire and it blazed up higher.

'Now this is what I'm going to do,' said the Magic Snowman. 'I'm going to take this nice little cottage for my own – and I shall live here. All of you others can live in a snow-house and freeze, for all I care. You will all wait on me and do whatever I say.'

'Yes,' said everybody. They all knew now what Moon-Face's plan was. He meant to make the room so hot that the Magic Snowman would melt. Clever old Moon-Face! A little trickle of water began to run from the Snowman's broad white back, which was near the fire. Moon-Face pointed to it secretly and grinned.

Frannie thought Moon-Face's beaming face looked so funny that she began to giggle. She really couldn't help it. Goldilocks giggled too, and stuffed her handkerchief into her small mouth. The baby bear gave a high squeak of a giggle.

'How dare you laugh!' shouted the Snowman angrily. 'Outside, all of you! Outside! This is my cottage now, and not one of you shall stay here.'

They all crowded outside except Moon-Face, who crouched behind a big chair, determined not to leave the fire in case it burnt low.

Outside it was bitterly cold. The white bears quickly dug up the snow and made a high wall to shelter the others from the wind. They crouched there, cuddling close to one another for warmth. The big white bears wrapped their furry arms round the children and warmed them beautifully. Joe thought they were very kind indeed.

They waited and they waited. They could see smoke pouring from the chimney of the cottage and they knew that Moon-Face must be keeping up the fire. The bears ooomphed every now and again, and the children whispered to one another.

Then suddenly the door of the cottage was flung open and Moon-Face stood there, his big face beaming like a full moon.

'You can come back now!' he shouted. 'It's quite safe!'

They all crowded back to the cottage. Joe looked for the Snowman – but he was gone! There was nothing to show that he had been there, except for a very large puddle of water.

'He melted very quickly,' said Moon-Face. 'He may have been very magic and very powerful – but he was just made of snow after all. So he melted like a real snowman on a sunny morning.'

The polar bears ooomphed with delight. They had hated being servants to the Snowman.

'We'll all say goodbye to you now,' they said to the Three Bears. 'This cottage is cosy but it's too hot for us. Come and see us again whenever you like. Goodbye!'

Everyone hugged them goodbye, and Joe felt quite sad to see them go. Moon-Face shut the door after them.

'Now we'll get back home,' he said. 'I'm a bit tired of this land. Come on, Bears, help me to get the cottage back safely!'

He didn't do the same magic as before. He drew a circle on the floor in blue chalk and the Three Bears stood inside, holding paws. Moon-Face danced around them, singing strings of odd magic words. A wind rose up, and the cottage rocked. Darkness came down, and for a moment no one could see anything at all.

Then gradually the darkness went and the wind blew no more. The sun shone warmly in at the window. Beth gave a shout.

'I say! We're back in the little woody corner where we first saw the cottage! And it's daytime now, not night-time!'

'Well, we've been having this adventure all night long!' said Moon-Face, with a laugh. 'It's sunrise now – the night has gone. You'd better hurry off home, children, or you'll be scolded for leaving your beds at night.'

They hugged Goldilocks, and shook hands with the Three Bears. 'We'll come back and see you sometime,' said Frannie. 'Thank you so much for all your help!'

Goldilocks and the bears stood at the door and waved goodbye as Moon-Face hurried the three children away down the lane to catch the train back to the Enchanted Wood. It wasn't long before they had got to the station, waited for a train, slid off the roof and settled down in a carriage.

When they got to the Enchanted Wood they said goodbye to Moon-Face, and Frannie gave him a kiss for being such a help. He was so pleased that he went red all over his enormous face, and Beth laughed.

'You look like the setting sun now,' she said. 'You really ought to be called Sun-Face!'

'Goodbye, and see you soon, I hope!' called Moon-Face. Off went the children home, and got into bed just about an hour before their mother called them to get up. My goodness, they *were* sleepy all that day!

XIII. MOON-FACE GETS INTO TROUBLE

The children didn't really feel that they wanted to go to any of the lands at the top of the Faraway Tree for a little while. It was a bit too exciting to climb through the clouds and see what was above them!

But they did want to see their friends in the Tree, especially dear old Moon-Face.

So the very next time they had a day to themselves they set off through the Enchanted Wood to the Faraway Tree. There was no rope to guide them this time. It was only at night that the rope was swung through the boughs to help the woodland-folk up and down.

The children began to climb up. Every door and window in the tree seemed shut today, and not a soul was about. It was quite dull climbing up the tree. Even when they reached Silky's house, that was shut too, and they couldn't hear Silky singing or anything. They knocked, but there was no answer.

So on they went up to Moon-Face's, keeping a good lookout for Dame Washalot's dirty water to come swishing down on them. But not even her water appeared that day! It all seemed very quiet and peaceful.

They reached Moon-Face's house at the top of the tree and knocked at his door. Nobody opened it.

But inside they could quite well hear somebody crying. It was very mysterious.

'It doesn't sound like Moon-Face,' said Frannie, puzzled. 'Let's go in and see who it is.'

So they opened the door and went in. And it was Silky, sitting in a corner crying bitterly!

'Whatever's the matter?' cried Joe.

'And where's old Moon-Face?' asked Frannie.

'Oh dear!' sobbed Silky. 'Moon-Face has been thrown into some dreadfully strange land at the top of the Faraway Tree because he was rude to Mister Watzisname down below.'

'What! That old man who's always sitting in a chair and snoring?' said Beth, remembering that they hadn't seen him that day. 'Whatever did Moon-Face do?'

'Oh, he was very naughty,' wept Silky. 'So was I. You see, we heard Mister Watzisname snoring as usual, and we crept up to him and saw that his mouth was wide open. And, oh dear, we popped a handful of acorns into it, and when he woke up he spluttered and popped, and then he caught sight of us hiding behind a big branch.'

'Goodness! Did you really dare to do such a naughty thing?' cried Beth. 'No wonder he was angry!'

'Moon-Face is dreadfully bad sometimes,' said Silky, wiping her eyes. 'He makes me naughty too. Well, we ran away up the tree to Moon-Face's house. I got in safely – but Moon-Face didn't. And Mister Watzisname caught hold of him and threw him right through the hole in the clouds into the land that is there today.'

'Good gracious! Well, can't he get back?' said Frannie, in alarm. 'He can climb down the ladder, surely, back into the Tree?'

'Yes, he could,' said Silky, 'but, you see, Mister Watzisname is sitting on the ladder ready to catch him and throw him back. So what's the use of that?'

'What land is up there today?' asked Joe.

'The Land of the Old Saucepan Man,' said Silky. 'He lives there in his cottage with his pots and pans, and is quite harmless. But, you see, Mister Watzisname will sit on the ladder till the land swings round and another one comes. Then Moon-Face won't be able to get back, and he may be lost forever!'

'Oh dear!' said Joe in dismay, and the girls stared at Silky in despair, for they were very fond of old Moon-Face now.

'Isn't there anything we can do?' asked Joe at last.

'Well, there's just one hope,' said Silky, fluffing out her lovely golden hair. 'The Old Saucepan Man is a great friend of Mister Watzisname's. If he knew his land was at the top of the Faraway Tree today he might come along and have a cup of tea with Mister Watzisname, and then Moon-Face could slip down the ladder back here!'

'Oh,' said the children, and looked at one another. They could quite well see that this meant one or all of them going up the ladder again and getting into another peculiar land.

'I'll go,' said Beth. 'After all, Moon-Face helped us last time. We must help him now.'

'We'll all three go,' said Joe. So they set off up the topmost branch to the little ladder. There they found Mister Watzisname sitting reading his newspaper and brewing a pot of tea that sent swirls of steam up through the hole in the clouds.

'Please can we pass?' asked Beth timidly.

'No, you can't,' said Mister Watzisname rudely.

'Well, we've got to,' said Joe. 'So if we tread on your feet you must excuse us.'

Mister Watzisname simply wouldn't move. He really was a very cross old man. He grumbled and growled at each of the children as they squeezed past him, and they were very glad when they had climbed through the hole and were in the land above.

'So this is the Land of the Saucepan Man,' said Frannie, when they were standing on the grass safely. 'What a funny little land!'

It was. It was an island floating in what seemed a sea of white. It wasn't really much bigger than a large field. Beth went to the edge and looked over.

'Goodness!' she said in alarm. 'It's like a cliff – and the sea is a big white cloud. Don't go too near the edge, anybody. It wouldn't be nice to fall off!'

'Hey! Hey!' suddenly yelled an excited voice. They turned around – and saw Moon-Face waving to them, and running hard towards them. 'Hey! How did you get here?'

'Hallo! We came to see what we could do for you,' said Joe. 'We heard what had happened. Old Mister Watzisname is sitting on the ladder still, waiting for you. But Silky says this is the land of the Saucepan Man, who is a great friend of Mister Watzisname's – so we've come to see him and ask him if he'll go and have tea with his friend. Then you can slip down safely and go home.'

'Ooooh, good!' said Moon-Face joyfully. 'I didn't know what land this was, and goodness me, I was quite afraid of falling off it, it's so small. Where do you suppose the Old Saucepan Man lives?'

'I can't imagine!' said Joe, looking round. All he could see was a very large stretch of grass, with no house and nobody at all in sight. Where in the world could the Saucepan Man live?

'We'll have to go carefully all round this funny little land,' said Beth. 'His house must be somewhere. But we'd better hurry, for you never know when the land will swing away from the Faraway Tree – and we don't want to live in this odd little place for ever!'

They began to walk round the land. Presently they came to a cliff that was not quite so steep as the others. They peered over it. Joe pointed to some things stuck in the cliff.

'Whatever are those?' he said.

'They look like some sort of steps down the cliffside,' said Beth.

'They're *saucepans*!' said Frannie suddenly. 'Yes – *saucepans* – with their handles stuck firmly into the cliff, and the pan part to tread on. How strange!'

'Well, this must be the way down to the Saucepan Man's house,' said Joe, excited. 'Come on. Be careful, girls, or you may fall and roll right over the edge of this land.'

So, very carefully, they began to climb down the cliff, treading on the saucepans stuck into the earth. It was really rather funny!

They got down at last. And then they heard a very curious noise indeed! It was a sound of crashings and bangings and clatterings and clangings! The children were quite alarmed.

'The noise is coming from just round the corner,' said Joe.

They crept very cautiously to the corner and peeped round.

There they saw a crooked little house with a saucepan for a chimney. The noise came from inside the house. The children crept to the window and looked in.

And inside they saw the strangest little man they had ever seen, dancing the strangest little dance! He had saucepans and kettles hung all over him, he wore a saucepan for a hat, and he crashed two saucepans together as he danced!

'Do you think he's dangerous?' said Joe, in a whisper.

XIV. THE FUNNY OLD SAUCEPAN MAN

'I don't think he's at all dangerous,' said Frannie. 'He has quite a kind face.'

'Let's tap at the window,' said Beth. So she tapped. But the Saucepan Man took no notice. He just went on dancing away, crashing his saucepans together.

Joe tapped loudly. The Saucepan Man caught sight of him at the window and looked most astonished. He stopped dancing and went to the door.

'Come in and dance,' he said.

'Oh no, thank you,' said Joe. 'We've just come to ask you to tea.'

'Ask me for a bee?' said the Saucepan Man, looking surprised. 'I'm so sorry, but I don't keep bees, only saucepans.'

'Not bees,' said Joe. 'To ask you out to TEA.'

'But I don't want to go to the sea,' said the Saucepan Man. 'I don't like the water at all. Never did. Very kind of you, I'm sure, but I hate the sea.'

'Not the sea, but TEA, TEA, TEA!' cried Joe.

'Oh, tea,' said the Saucepan Man. 'Well, why didn't you say that before? Then I would have understood.'

'I *did* say that before,' said poor Joe.

'What? Shut the door?' said the Saucepan Man. 'Certainly, if you want to. Give it a push.'

'He can't hear very well,' said Frannie. 'He must be deaf.'

'No, I'm not,' said the Saucepan Man, hearing perfectly all of a sudden. 'Not a bit deaf. Only sometimes when my saucepans have been crashing round me rather a lot I get noises in my ears afterwards. But I'm not deaf.'

'I'm glad of that,' said Joe politely.

'Cat? No, I haven't got a cat,' said the Saucepan Man, looking all round. 'Did you see one?'

'I didn't say anything about a cat,' said Joe patiently.

'You did. I heard you,' said the Saucepan Man, vexed. 'I don't encourage cats. I keep mice instead. I shall look for that cat.'

And then, with his saucepans clanging round him he began to look for a cat that certainly wasn't there. 'Puss, Puss, Puss!' he called. 'Puss, Puss, Puss!'

'There's no cat in your house!' shouted Moon-Face.

'Mouse? Where did you see you a mouse?' said the old man, alarmed. 'I wouldn't like one of my mice to be caught by your cat.'

'I tell you we haven't GOT a cat!' cried Joe, feeling quite cross. 'We've come to tell you about your friend, Mister Watzisname.'

For once the Saucepan Man seemed to hear Joe, and at once he stopped looking for the cat. 'Mister Watzisname!' he cried. 'Where is he? He's a great friend of mine.'

'Well, wouldn't you like to go and have tea with him then?' said Joe.

'Yes, certainly I would,' said the Saucepan Man. 'Please tell me where he is.'

'He's sitting on the ladder leading from the Faraway Tree to your land,' shouted Joe. 'He's waiting there.'

'Yes – for me!' said Moon-Face in a whisper.

'Ssh!' said Frannie. The Saucepan Man gave a yell of joy when he heard where his old friend was, and he set off for the cliff, shouting in delight.

'Hurrah! I've come to the Faraway Tree! And I can see my friends again! And Mister Watzisname is waiting for me to have tea with him! Come on! Come on!'

Up the cliff he went, treading on the saucepan steps, his own saucepans and kettles rattling and banging all round him. The children and Moon-Face followed. The Saucepan Man ran helter-skelter to the hole that led down to the topmost branch of the Faraway Tree, dropping a few saucepans on the way.

When he got there he peered down and saw Mister Watzisname sitting on the ladder, watching for Moon-Face. But the Saucepan Man didn't know that, of course! He thought that his friend was waiting for *him*!

'Hey, hey, hey!' he yelled, dropping a saucepan on top of Mister Watzisname in his excitement. 'Hey, old friend!'

Mister Watzisname watched the saucepan bouncing off his foot, down the branch of the Faraway Tree, and wondered who it would hit. He looked up in amazement when he heard his friend's shouts.

'Saucepan!' he yelled. 'Dear old Saucepan! Fancy seeing *you*!'

'Glue?' said the Saucepan Man, suddenly hearing all wrong again. 'Glue? – No – I've not got glue with me. But I can soon make some for you.'

'Still the same silly old Saucepan Man, aren't you!' cried Mister Watzisname. 'Come down here. I didn't say anything about glue. Come and have a cup of tea

81

with me. The kettle's boiling.'

'I don't want oiling,' said the Saucepan Man, though he really sounded as if he did, he was so full of clangs and clatters! 'I'll come and have tea and a talk with you. Hurrah!'

He put his foot on the ladder, but unfortunately he stepped on a kettle that had got round his leg, and down he went, clatter, bang, crash, smash, clang! Mister Watzisname caught at him as he went past, and down he went too, rolling off the ladder, down the branch, past Moon-Face's door and down the Tree!

'There they go!' said Moon-Face, in delight. 'All mixed up with kettles and saucepans. What a joke! They'll give old Dame Washalot a fright if they fall into her wash-tub!'

The children laughed till they cried. The Old Saucepan Man was really so funny, and they couldn't *imagine* what people in the Tree would think as he rolled down with such a clanging and banging.

'It's quite safe to go down now,' said Joe, peering down the ladder. 'They've disappeared. I shouldn't wonder if they're at the bottom of the Tree by now. Come on, Moon-Face.'

So down the ladder they all went, slid down the topmost branch, and opened Moon-Face's door. Silky was still there, looking scared out of her life. She gave a scream of joy when she saw them.

'Why are you looking so frightened?' asked Moon-Face, giving her a hug.

'Oh, goodness, a thunderbolt or something fell out of the sky just now and rolled crashing down the Tree!' said Silky.

'That was only the Saucepan Man and Mister Watzisname,' said Joe, laughing, and he told her the whole story. Silky laughed till her sides ached. She ran out of the door and peeped down the Tree.

'Look!' she said, pointing. 'Can you see far down there, between the branches?'

They all looked – and they saw Mister Watzisname and the Old Saucepan Man climbing painfully up to Mister Watzisname's home, both talking together at the top of their voices.

'They've forgotten all about us,' said Joe joyfully. 'Now for goodness' sake, Moon-Face, don't go putting acorns into Mister Watzisname's mouth again. Let's have something to eat, and then we must go home down your slippery-slip.'

So they all five sat round Moon-Face's funny room and ate some Pop Cakes that Silky fetched, and drank acornade, which was made of acorns and was most delicious. Then it was time for the children to go, and they chose cushions, sat at the top of the big tree-slide, pushed off and flew down the inside of the tree, sliding round and round and round till they shot out of the trapdoor at the bottom on to the cushion of moss. Then they ran home as fast as they could, for they were late.

'I expect the Old Saucepan Man's gone back to his odd little land by now,' said Joe, as they turned in at their gate.

But he hadn't. He came to see them the very next

day, his saucepans clanging so loudly that Mother looked quite alarmed.

'Whoever in the world is that?' she said, as the Saucepan Man came in at the gate.

XV. THE SAUCEPAN MAN GOES TO THE WRONG LAND!

Mother and the children stared at the strange Old Saucepan Man as he came in at the gate. He wore an extra-large-sized saucepan for a hat, and, as he came, he knocked two pans together, and sang an odd nonsense song that went like this:

> 'Two beans for a pudding,
> Two cherries for a pie,
> Two legs for a table,
> With a hi-diddle-hi !'

At the last 'hi' he banged on the door with a saucepan. Mother opened it.

'Don't make such a noise,' she said.

'No, I haven't seen any boys,' said the Saucepan Man, and he clashed his pans together so loudly that Mother jumped. Then he caught sight of the children and waved to them eagerly. 'Oh, there you are! Moon-Face told me where you lived.'

'Whoever is he?' said Mother, in wonder. 'Children, is this strange old man all right?'

'Oh yes,' said Joe, hoping that Mother wouldn't ask them too many questions. 'Can we take him into the garden, Mother? He makes such a noise indoors.'

'Very well,' said Mother, who wanted to get on with her washing. 'Take him along.'

'A song?' said the Saucepan Man obligingly. 'Did you say you wanted a song, Madam?' He began to sing again, and crashed his pans in time to his song:

'Two pigs for the pigsty,
Two shoes for the horse,
Two hats for the tigers,
Pink ones, of course.'

The children bustled him out into the back-garden. 'That's a very, very silly song of yours,' said Beth loudly, right in his ear. 'What's it called?'

'It hasn't got a name,' said the Saucepan Man. 'I make it up as I go along. It's quite easy. Every line but the last one begins with the word 'two'. I'm sorry you think it's silly.' He looked rather offended. Then suddenly he smiled again and said, 'I've come to ask you all to tea in my cottage.'

'Will Mister Watzisname be there?' asked Joe, who wasn't at all keen to meet him again.

'Yes, you'd better brush your hair,' said the Saucepan Man, looking at Joe's untidy hair.

'I said 'Will Mister Watzisname be there?'' said Joe, loudly.

'Something in the air?' said the Saucepan Man, and he looked up anxiously. 'Not a thunderstorm, I hope?'

'No, I certainly don't mean a thunderstorm,' said Joe, with a groan. 'Yes – we'll come. We must ask Mother first.'

Mother said they could go, though she still thought that Old Saucepan Man was very loud and annoying.

'Good day,' she said to him, as he and the children

went off.

He really was a most peculiar sight, but he had such a twinkly sort of face that the three children couldn't help liking him and trusting him.

They soon came to the Faraway Tree, and saw that Moon-Face had thought of a marvellous idea. He had borrowed Dame Washalot's biggest washing basket and let it down on a rope. Then, as soon as they were all safely in it, he and Silky meant to haul them up, to save them the long, long climb!

'That's a really good idea!' said Joe, delighted. They all climbed in. It was a bit difficult to get the Saucepan Man in too, but they managed at last, though he seemed to find it most uncomfortable to sit on his saucepans.

'Up we go!' shouted Joe as the basket swung upwards through the branches. It ran very smoothly, and the children enjoyed the strange ride. At last they came to a big branch and stepped out on it. It was quite near Moon-Face's house at the top. Moon-Face was there, winding up the rope, a grin on his big, shining face.

'How did you like *that*?' he asked. The Saucepan Man looked at him anxiously.

'Cat?' he said. 'Another cat? Dear me! I hope it won't escape into my land. I've got my mice there.'

'Now he'll go looking for cats again,' said Beth. And sure enough the Saucepan Man began to peer here and there, calling, 'Puss, Puss, Puss!'

'Never mind him,' said Moon-Face. 'Go on up the ladder. He wants you to go to tea with him in his funny saucepanny house!'

'Come on, Saucepan Man!' called Joe. 'If you want us to come to tea, we'd better go!'

The Saucepan Man heard. He stopped looking for cats and ran up the ladder. With a bound he was through the hole in the cloud, and right above.

And no sooner had he gone out of sight than he began to yell:

'Ooooh! Oooohowww! Wowooo!'

The children listened in alarm. 'Whatever's the matter with him?' said Joe.

Crash! Bang! Clang! Smash!

'He sounds as if he's rolling about on all his kettles and saucepans!' said Beth. 'What can he be doing?'

'Ooooohooow!' shouted the Saucepan Man above them. 'Stop it! Ow! Stop it!'

'Somebody must be attacking him!' cried Joe. He leapt up the ladder. 'Come on, everyone! We'll soon send any enemies off!'

He shot up the ladder, followed by Beth, Frannie, and Moon-Face. They all clambered through the hole in the clouds and stood in the land above.

But oh, my goodness me! It was no longer the Land of the Saucepan Man, that tiny, little, cloud-edged country! It was another land altogether!

'My land's gone!' shrieked the Saucepan Man. 'I didn't know it had! This is somewhere else! Oooooh!'

No wonder he said 'Ooooh!' The bit of flat field he was standing on suddenly gave a shiver like a jelly, and then just as suddenly tipped itself up so that it made a hill! The Saucepan Man rolled down it at top speed, all his pans clattering like cymbals!

'This is Rocking Land,' said Moon-Face, in dismay. 'Quick! Come back to the ladder and get down the hole before we have forgotten where it is! Hey, Saucepan Man, come over here to us!'

'Bus, did you say?' shouted back the Saucepan Man, picking himself up and looking round. 'I can't see a bus. I'd like to catch one.'

'Come here to US, to US, to US!' shouted Joe, in despair. 'The hole through the clouds is here. We must get back again quickly!'

The Saucepan Man began to run downhill to them, but the ground all round suddenly tipped backwards, and he and the children and Moon-Face found themselves running downhill away from the hole in the clouds, where the precious ladder was! They tried to stop. They tried to walk back up the sudden hill – but the land tipped up all the more and in the end they couldn't stand up, but had to lie down.

Then they began to roll downhill. How they rolled!

Over and over and over and over, with the Saucepan Man making a dreadful clatter with all his pans.

'Oooooh! Ow! Oooooh!' cried everyone.

'We've lost the hole!' shouted Joe. But before he could say any more he bumped into a bush that knocked all the breath out of him! Soon everyone lay in a heap at the bottom of the hill, and tried to get back their breath.

'Now we're in a fix,' said Beth, dusting herself. 'What a very tiresome land to have got into. Does it do this sort of thing all the time, Moon-Face?'

'Oh, yes,' said Moon-Face. 'It never stops. It heaves up here and sinks down there, and rocks to and fro and gives sudden little jumps. People do say there's a giant just underneath, trying to throw the land off his back.'

XVI. WHAT HAPPENED IN
THE ROCKING LAND

The Rocking Land was really most annoying. No sooner did the children stand up very carefully and try to walk a few steps, than the earth beneath them either fell away or tipped up or slanted sideways in a very alarming manner.

Then down they all went, rolling over and over! The Saucepan Man made a tremendous noise and almost cried when he saw how battered his saucepans and kettles were getting.

'Moon-Face!' yelled Joe. 'How can we get out of here? Don't you know?'

'We can only get out by going down the ladder that leads to the Faraway Tree!' shouted back Moon-Face, who was busy rolling down a little hill that had suddenly appeared. 'Look for it all the time, or we'll never get away from here. As soon as the Rocking Land leaves the place where the Faraway Tree is, we've no way of escape!'

That gave the others a shock. The thought of living in a land of bumps and jolts was not at all pleasant! They all began to look about for the hole through which they had come into the Rocking Land.

Soon the earth began to do something very different. It heaved up and down very quickly as if it were breathing fast! When it heaved up it threw the children and the others into the air. When it breathed downwards they rolled into holes and stayed there. It was all dreadfully uncomfortable.

'I'm getting awfully bruised!' shouted Beth. 'For goodness' sake let's find a place on this land where it's not quite so fidgety. I think we must be on the worst bit.'

As soon as the earth stopped heaving about they all ran hard to where a wood grew. And there, just inside the wood, they saw a shop!

It was such a surprising thing to see in the Rocking Land that they all stopped and stared.

'What does it sell?' said Joe.

'You don't feel *well*?' said the Saucepan Man, quite deaf for a time. 'I don't either. I feel as if I've been on a ship in a very rough sea!'

'I said, "What does the shop *sell*?"' said Joe.

'No, I didn't hear a bell,' said the Saucepan Man, looking round as if he expected to see an enormous bell somewhere.

Joe gave up. He looked hard at the shop. It was just a wide stall, with a tiny house behind it. No one seemed to be there, but smoke rose from the chimney, so someone must live there, Joe thought.

'Come on,' he said to the others. 'Take hold of each others' hands, so that we keep together. We'll go and see this funny shop and see if we can get help.'

They walked up to it. The stall was piled high with cushions of all colours, each one with a rope tied to it.

'How funny!' said Beth, in astonishment. 'Cushions with ropes! Now who in the world would want to buy cushions here?'

'Well, I would, for one!' said Moon-Face at once. 'My goodness, if I had a fine fat cushion tied on the front of me, and another tied at the back, I wouldn't mind being bumped around nearly so much!'

'Oh, of course – that's what the cushions and ropes are for,' said Beth joyfully. 'Let's buy some – then we shan't get bruised any more.'

Just then a sharp-nosed little woman, with cushions tied all round her, came out of the tiny house and looked at the children. She even had a small cushion tied on her head, and she did look funny.

Frannie giggled. She was a dreadful giggler. The woman looked cross and glared at Frannie.

'Do you want to buy my cushions?' she asked.

'Yes please,' said Moon-Face, and he reached into his pocket. 'How much are they?'

'Five silver pieces of money each,' said the woman, her little green eyes shining as she saw Moon-Face putting his hand into his pocket for the money. Moon-Face looked at her in dismay.

'That's much too high a price!' he said. 'I've only got one silver piece. Have you got any money, Saucepan Man?'

'No, I don't sell honey,' said the Saucepan Man.

'MONEY, MONEY, MONEY!' shouted Moon-Face, showing the Saucepan Man his one silver piece.

'Oh, money,' he said, taking out a round leather bag from one of his kettles. 'Yes, I've plenty in here.'

But the round leather bag was empty! The Saucepan Man stared at it in dismay.

'All my money must have fallen out when I rolled about,' he said. 'There's nothing left!'

The children had no money at all. The sharp-nosed little woman shook her head when Moon-Face begged her to lend them some cushions in return for his silver piece.

'I don't lend anything,' she said, and went back to her house, banging the door loudly.

'It's too bad,' said Moon-Face, taking hold of Joe's hand and walking off gloomily. 'Mean old thing! Oh, look – there are some more people – all wearing cushions!'

Sure enough they met plenty of odd-looking folk, well-padded with cushions of all colours, sizes and shapes, walking carefully about the paths. One man wore a big quilt all round him, which Beth thought was a fine idea.

'The Rocking Land is quite peaceful for a change,' she said to Frannie. But she spoke too soon – for even as she said these words the earth began to heave up, first one way and then another!

Over went the children and everybody else and rolled here and there and up and down as the land jumped up first in one place and then in another.

'Ooooooh!' groaned the children.

'Wish I had a few cushions!' cried Moon-Face, who had rolled on his nose and bent it sideways.

Crash! Clank! Bang! went the Saucepan Man, rolling on his kettles and pans very noisily.

'Oooh, look!' shrieked Beth suddenly, in delight, and pointed back towards the little wood where the shop was. The earth there had risen steeply upwards, and all the cushions were rolling down towards the children.

'Grab them!' shouted Joe. So they all caught the cushions, and began to tie them firmly round them. My goodness, it did make a difference when they rolled about!

'It serves that mean old woman right!' said the Saucepan Man as he tried his hardest to put cushions round himself and his saucepans.

Suddenly one of the people of the Rocking Land gave a frightened shout and clutched hold of a nearby tree. A strange wind blew with a low, musical sound.

'Now what's going to happen?' cried Moon-Face.

'Get hold of a tree! Get hold of a tree!' shouted the people round about. 'When the wind makes that sound it means the whole of the land is going to tip up sideways and try to roll everyone off. Your only hope is to catch hold of a tree!'

Sure enough, the land was tipping up – not in bits and pieces as it had done before, but the whole of it! It was extraordinary. Moon-Face was frightened. He tried to get to a tree, and he shouted to the others.

'Catch hold of a tree! Hurry up!'

But not one of them could, for they had left the wood behind them and were in a field. Slowly and surely the land tipped sideways, and the children and Moon-Face and the old Saucepan Man began to roll downhill on their cushions. They were not bruised, but they were very much frightened. What would happen to them if they rolled right off the land?

Down they went and down, nearer and nearer to the edge of the Rocking Land – and then, quite suddenly, Moon-Face disappeared! One moment he was there – the next he was gone! It was most peculiar.

But in half a minute they heard his voice, lifted up in the greatest excitement. 'I say, I say, everyone! I've fallen down the hole to the ladder that leads to the Faraway Tree, quite by accident. I'll throw my cushions up through the hole so you'll know where it is. Roll to it if you can! But hurry!'

Then the children and the Saucepan Man saw two cushions appear, and they knew where the hole was. They did their best to roll to it, and one by one they got nearer and nearer.

Beth rolled right down it, plop, and caught hold of the ladder as she fell. Joe rolled down next, missed the ladder and landed with a bump on the top branch of the Faraway Tree.

The Saucepan Man rolled to it next, but he got stuck in the hole, for he was now so fat with cushions as well as kettles and saucepans that he could hardly get through.

'Oh, quick, quick, quick!' shouted Joe. 'Get in, Saucepan Man, get in! Poor Frannie will roll right past the hole if you don't hurry up!'

The Saucepan Man saw Frannie was rolling past. Poor Frannie! Once she rolled past the hole she couldn't possibly roll back again, for it would be all uphill. Quick as lightning the Saucepan Man reached out his hand and caught hold of one of the ropes that tied Frannie's cushion to her back. She stopped with a jerk.

One of the Saucepan Man's kettles gave way and he fell through the hole to the ladder, making a tremendous noise. Moon-Face caught him – and then the Saucepan Man gave a tug at Frannie's rope and she came down the hole too, landing softly on the top branch of the Faraway Tree, for she was well-padded with her cushions!

'Well, thank goodness you found the hole, Moon-Face!' said everyone, still looking rather scared. '*What an adventure!*'

XVII. AN INVITATION FROM MOON-FACE AND SILKY

Nobody had really enjoyed their visit to the Rocking Land, which had been a mistake, anyhow. They sat in Moon-Face's house, untying their cushions from their backs and fronts, and looking at all the bruises they had got.

'What shall we do with these cushions?' said Beth.

'Moon-Face could do with them, I expect,' said Frannie. 'He uses such a lot for his slippery-slip, don't you, Moon-Face?'

'Yes, they'd do very well,' said Moon-Face, his big face beaming joyfully. 'Some of mine are getting very old and worn. We can't possibly give them back to that cross old woman in the Rocking Land, so we might as well put them to some use here.'

'Right,' said Joe, and he handed Moon-Face his two cushions. Everyone else did the same. Moon-Face was pleased. He poured lemonade for everyone, then handed round a little box full of what looked like all sorts of toffee.

'I don't feel as if I ever want to see what land is at the top of the Faraway Tree again,' said Joe, as he munched a peculiar piece of toffee which seemed to get bigger in his mouth instead of smaller.

'Neither do I,' said Beth.

'I certainly never will!' said Frannie. 'It seems as if there are never any lands there worth visiting. They are all most uncomfortable.'

'Except *my* little land,' said the Saucepan Man, rather mournfully. 'I was always very comfortable there.'

Joe's toffee was now so big that he couldn't say a word. Then it suddenly exploded in his mouth, went to nothing, and left him feeling most astonished.

'Oh dear – did you take a Toffee Shock?' said Moon-Face, noticing Joe's surprised face. 'I'm so sorry. Take a different one.'

'No, thank you,' said Joe, feeling that one Toffee Shock was quite enough. 'I think we'd really better be going. It must be getting late.'

'What's going to happen to the old Saucepan Man now that he's lost his land?' asked Beth, picking up a yellow cushion, ready to slide down the tree.

'Oh, he'll live with Mister Watzisname,' said Moon-Face. 'Hallo – he's taken a Toffee Shock by mistake. Oh, *do* watch him!'

They all watched. The Saucepan Man's Toffee Shock had got enormous, and was about to explode. It did – and went back down to nothing again in his mouth. The Saucepan Man blinked his eyes and looked so astonished that everyone shouted with laughter.

'That was a Toffee Shock you were eating!' said Moon-Face.

'A Coffee Clock?' said the Saucepan Man, even more surprised. 'Dear me!'

'Come on!' said Beth, giggling. 'It's time we went. See you another day, Moon-Face! Goodbye, Saucepan Man!'

She shot off down the slide, round and round and out of the trapdoor at the bottom. Then Frannie slid off, and then Joe.

'Goodbye,' he called. 'Goodbye!'

Mother was astonished to see their bruises. 'Whatever have you been doing?' she said. 'I shan't let you play with the Saucepan Man again if you come home like this. And how dirty your clothes are!'

Joe longed to tell Mother about the Rocking Land and their adventure there, but he felt sure she would think he was making it all up. So he said nothing and went off to change his dirty clothes.

Things did not go very well the next week. Father lost some money one night, and Mother could not get very much washing to do. So money was very scarce, and the children did not have as much to eat as they would have liked.

'If only we could have a few hens!' sighed Mother. 'They would at least give us eggs to eat. And a little goat would give us milk.'

'And what I want is a new garden shovel,' said Father. 'Mine broke yesterday and I can't get on with the garden. It's very important that we should grow as many vegetables as possible, for we can't afford to buy them!'

To make things worse their father was very cross with them for having spoilt their clothes the day that they had gone off with the Saucepan Man.

'If that's the way you treat the only nice clothes you have, you will just have to stay at home and not go out at all!' he scolded.

The children did not like being scolded, and Beth mended their clothes as nicely as she could. Two weeks went by, and the children had not even had two hours to themselves to go and see Moon-Face.

'He'll be wondering what has happened to us,' said Frannie.

Moon-Face certainly *was* wondering. He had waited each day and each night to see the children, and he and Silky wondered what was the matter.

'We'll send the Barn Owl with a note to tell the children to come quickly,' said Silky at last. So she slipped down the Faraway Tree to the hole where the Barn Owl lived. She knocked at his door, and he pecked it open.

'What is it?' he asked in a hoarse voice.

'Oh, Barny dear, will you take this note to the children at that little cottage over by the wood?' asked Silky, in her sweetest voice. 'You're going out hunting tonight, aren't you?'

'Yes,' said the Barn Owl, and he took the note in one of his great clawed feet. 'I'll take it.'

He slammed the door shut behind him and rose into the air on great creamy wings, as silent as the wind. He flew to the children's cottage. They were in bed, asleep.

Barny sat on the tree outside and screeched loudly. The children awoke with a jump.

'Whatever's that?' said Beth.

Joe came into the room. 'Did you hear that?' he asked. 'Whatever could it be?'

The Barn Owl screeched again. He certainly had a

101

dreadful voice. The children jumped. Joe went bravely to the window and looked out. 'Is anyone being hurt?' he called.

'Meeeeeeee!' screeched the owl again, and Joe nearly fell out of the window with fright! The Barn Owl spread his great soft wings and flew to Joe. He dropped the note on to the window-sill, screeched again, and flew off into the night to look for mice and rats.

'It was a Barn Owl!' said Joe. 'It left a note! Quick, turn on your bedside lamp and let's see what the letter says!'

They turned the lamp on and crowded round the note. This is what it said:

'DEAR JOE, BETH, AND FRANNIE,
Why don't you come to see us? Are you upset? Please come soon, because there is a wonderful land at the top of the Tree now. It is the Land of Take-What-You-Want. If you want anything, you can usually get it there for nothing. Do come, and we'll all go together. Love from
MOON-FACE AND SILKY.'

'Ooooh!' said Frannie, excited. 'The Land of Take-What-You-Want! Well, *I'd* like to get a few hens.'

'And *I'd* like a goat!' said Beth.

'And *I'd* like a new shovel for Father!' said Joe.

But then he frowned. 'I'd quite made up my mind not to go up to any more of those strange lands,' he said. 'You just never know what might happen there. We'd better not go.'

'Oh, *Joe*!' cried Beth. 'Please let's go! After all, if there *is* a nice land we might as well visit it.'

'Sssh! You'll wake up Mother!' said Joe. 'We'll see tomorrow what happens. If we can get some time to ourselves we'll go and ask Moon-Face if the land is really *safe* to go to. Now we'd better go to bed and sleep.'

But they didn't sleep much! No – they were all wondering what the Land of Take-What-You-Want was like, and if they were really going to visit it tomorrow!

XVIII. THE LAND OF TAKE-WHAT-YOU-WANT

The next day was very fine. The children helped their mother to clean the whole house, and Joe proudly brought in some fine green beans and lettuces from the garden, which he had grown himself. Mother was pleased.

'You can go off and play after lunch if you like,' she said. 'You have been very good today.'

The children looked at one another in glee. Just what they had hoped for! Good!

'Come on!' said Joe, after lunch. 'We won't waste any time!'

'What about something to drink?' said Beth. 'Shouldn't we take some lemonade with us?'

'I should think we can get lemonade all right from the Land of Take-What-You-Want!' said Joe, with a grin.

So they all ran off, waving to Mother as they went. They were soon in the Enchanted Wood, hearing the trees whispering secretly to one-another, 'Wisha-wisha-wisha!'

They ran through the bushes and trees to the Faraway Tree, and up they went. When they passed the window of the Angry Pixie, Joe peeped in, just for fun. But he was sorry he did, for the Angry Pixie was there, and he threw a bowl of cold soup all over poor Joe!

'Oh!' said Joe in dismay, as he saw his shirt all splashed with soup. 'You wicked pixie!'

The Angry Pixie went off into peals of delighted laughter, and banged his window shut.

'Pooh! You do smell of onions now, Joe!' said Beth, wrinkling up her nose. 'I hope the smell soon wears off.'

Joe wiped himself down with his handkerchief. He said to himself that one day he would pay the Angry Pixie back!

'Come on,' said Frannie impatiently. 'We'll never get there!'

They passed the Barn Owl's door and saw him sitting inside, fast asleep. They came to Silky's little yellow door too, but she wasn't in. There was a note pinned on her door which said, 'OUT. BACK SOON.'

'She must be with Moon-Face,' said Joe. 'Now just look out for Dame Washalot's water, everyone.'

It was a good thing he reminded them, for not long after that a fine waterfall of soapy suds came pouring down. Frannie screamed and dodged, so did Beth. Joe got some on his shirt and he was very cross.

'Never mind!' said Frannie, with a giggle. 'It will wash off some of the onion soup, Joe!'

They went on up, and came to Mister Watzisname's. He was, as usual, sitting in a deckchair, fast asleep, with his mouth open. And beside him, also fast asleep, was the Old Saucepan Man, looking most uncomfortable, draped round as usual with saucepans and kettles.

'Don't wake them,' whispered Joe. 'We'd better not

stop and talk.' So they crept by them – but just as they had got to the next branch the Saucepan Man woke up.

He sniffed hard, and jabbed Mister Watzisname. 'What's the matter, what's the matter?' said his friend.

'Can you smell onions?' asked the Saucepan Man. 'I distinctly smell them. Do you suppose the Faraway Tree is growing onions anywhere near us today? I love onion soup.'

Joe and the girls laughed till they cried. 'It's the onion soup on your shirt that the Saucepan Man smelt,' said Beth. 'My goodness! They'll spend all the afternoon looking for onions growing on the Faraway Tree!'

They left the two funny old men and went climbing up – and they got nicely caught by Dame Washalot's second lot of water. She was doing a great deal of washing that day, and she emptied a big wash-tub down just as the three children were nearly underneath.

'Slishy-sloshy-slishy-sloshy!' The water came pouring down and soaked all the children. They gasped and shook themselves like dogs. 'Quick!' said Joe. 'We will go as fast as we can to Moon-Face's house and borrow some towels from him. This is dreadful!'

They arrived at Moon-Face's at last. Old Moon-Face and Silky rushed out to hug them – but when they saw how dripping wet the children were, they stopped in surprise.

'Is it raining?' said Moon-Face.

'Have you had a bath in your clothes?' asked Silky.

'No. It's just Dame Washalot's water as usual,' said

Joe crossly. 'We dodged the first lot, but didn't manage to dodge the second lot. Can you lend us towels?'

Moon-Face grinned and pulled some towels out of his curved cupboard. As the children rubbed themselves down, Moon-Face told them all about the Land of Take-What-You-Want.

'It's a marvellous land,' he said. 'You are allowed to wander all over it and take whatever you want for yourselves without paying a penny. Everyone goes there if they can. Do come and visit it with me and Silky.'

'Is it quite, quite safe?' asked Joe, rubbing his hair dry.

'Oh yes,' said Silky. 'The only thing is we must be careful not to stay there too long, in case it leaves the Faraway Tree and we can't get down. But Moon-Face says he will sit by the ladder and give a loud whistle if he sees any sign of the Land moving away.'

'Good,' said Joe. 'Well, there are plenty of things we want. So let's go now, shall we?'

They all climbed up the topmost branch to the great white cloud. The ladder led through the hole as usual to the land above. One by one they climbed it and stood in the strange country above the magic cloud.

It was indeed strange! It was simply crowded with things and people! It was quite difficult to move about. Animals of all kinds wandered here and there; sacks of all sorts of things, from gold to potatoes, stood about; stalls of the most wonderful vegetables and fruit were everywhere; and even such things as chairs and tables were to be found waiting for anyone to take them!

'Good gracious!' said Joe. 'Can we really take anything we want?'

'Anything!' said Moon-Face, settling himself down by the ladder in the cloud. 'Look at those gnomes over there! They mean to take all the gold they can find!'

The children looked where Moon-Face was pointing. Sure enough there were four gnomes, hauling at all the sacks of gold in sight. One by one they staggered off to the ladder with them and disappeared down to the Faraway Tree. Other fairy folk hunted for the different things they wanted – dresses, coats, shoes, singing birds, pictures, all kinds of things! As soon as they had found what they were looking for, they rushed off to the ladder in glee and slipped down it. Moon-Face found it fun to watch them.

The others wandered off, looking at everything in surprise.

'Do you want a nice fat lion, Joe?' asked Silky, as a large lion wandered by and licked Silky's hand.

'No, thank you,' said Joe, at once.

'Well, what about a giraffe?' said Silky. 'I believe they make fine pets.'

'You believe wrong then,' said Beth, as a tall giraffe galloped past like a giant rocking horse. 'Nobody in their senses would want to keep a giraffe for a pet.'

'Oh look,' cried Frannie, as she came to a shop in which stood a great many large and beautiful clocks. 'Do let's take a clock back home!'

'No, thank you,' said Joe. 'We know what we want and we'll take that and nothing else.'

'I think *I* should like a clock,' said Silky, and she picked up a small clock with a very nice smiley face. It had two feet underneath, which wiggled hard as Silky picked up the clock.

'It wants to walk!' said Beth with a scream of laughter. 'Oh, do let it, Silky. I've never seen a clock walk before!'

Silky put the clock down and it trotted beside them on its big flat feet. The children thought it was the funniest thing they had ever seen. Silky was very pleased with her new clock. It was the kind that chimed every hour, on the hour, and sometimes in between too. And it had to be wound up with a key every night, to keep it ticking.

'Just what I've always wanted,' she said. 'I shall keep it at the back of my room.'

'You don't suppose it will stay there, do you, Silky?' asked Beth. 'It will wander round and about and poke its nose into everything you're doing. And if it doesn't like you it will run away!'

'Ding-dong-ding-dong!' said the clock suddenly, in

a clear voice, making them all jump. It stopped walking when it chimed, but it ran after the children and Silky again at once. It was really a most extraordinary clock!

'Now we really must look for what *we* want,' said Joe. 'Are those hens over there, Beth?'

'Yes, they are!' said Beth. 'Good! Come along and we'll get them. Oh, this is really a lovely land! I *am* glad we came! What fun it will be getting everything we want. I do wonder what Mother will say when we get home!'

XIX. MOON-FACE GETS INTO A FIX

The children went over to the hens that Joe had seen. They were lovely ones, but a very peculiar colour, for their wings were pale green and the rest of their feathers were buttercup yellow. They had funny high voices, and were very friendly indeed, for they came to press themselves round the children's legs like cats!

'Do you suppose Mother would like hens this colour?' asked Joe, doubtfully.

'I don't see why not,' said Beth. 'I think they are very pretty. The thing is – do they lay good eggs?'

One of the hens at once laid an egg. It was large and quite an ordinary colour. Beth was pleased.

'There you are!' she said. 'If they lay eggs as big as this one, Mother will be *very* pleased. How many hens are there – one, two, three, four, five, six, seven! I wonder how we could take them all.'

'Oh, they'll follow you,' said Silky. 'Just like my clock follows me! Tell them you want them and they'll come.'

'We want you to come with us, hens,' said Joe at once, and the seven green-winged birds came over to him and lined up in a row to follow the children. It was really very funny.

'Well, that's our hens found!' said Beth, pleased. 'Now for the goat and the shovel.'

They wandered along, looking at everything. It didn't matter what anyone wanted, they were sure to find it sooner or later! There were boats there, all kinds of dogs, shopping-baskets, rings, toys, work-baskets, and even such small things as thimbles!

'It's the strangest land I ever saw!' said Joe.

'We look pretty strange too!' said Frannie, giggling, as she looked round and saw the seven hens and the big clock padding along behind them. 'Oh, look – there's the dearest, prettiest white goat I ever saw! Do let's take her!'

Sure enough, not far off was a lovely white nanny-goat, with soft brown eyes and perky ears. She looked quite ordinary except for two blue spots by her tail.

'Little white goat, come with us!' cried Frannie, and the goat trotted up at once. It took its place behind the hens, but it didn't seem to like the clock, which bumped into it every now and again, just to tease it.

'Don't do that, clock,' said Silky.

'I hope your clock won't be a nuisance,' said Beth. 'I think it likes acting silly!'

'Now for the garden shovel,' said Joe, as he suddenly saw a fine strong shovel standing up against a fence with some other garden tools. 'What about this one, girls? This looks strong enough for Father, doesn't it?'

He took a hold of it and jabbed it into the ground. It was just the sight sort. Joe put it over his shoulder, and the four of them grinned happily at each other.

'We've got everything we want,' said Joe. 'Come on.

We'll go back to old Moon-Face and then we'll take some cakes to eat at home.'

So, followed by the seven hens, the white goat, and the clock, the four of them made their way back to where they had left Moon-Face. But he wasn't sitting where they had left him. He was pulling at a lovely rug, which was hanging from a tree. It was perfectly round, with a hole in the middle.

'Hallo, hallo!' yelled Moon-Face, as he saw them. 'Look what I've got! Just what I've always wanted for my round tree room – a round rug with a hole in the middle where the slippery-slip begins! Wonderful!'

'But, Moon-Face, you said you'd watch to see that the Land of Take-What-You-Want kept by the Faraway Tree alright, didn't you?' said Silky anxiously. 'Where is the hole that leads down to the tree?'

'Oh, it's somewhere over there,' said Moon-Face, draping the rug round him and staggering off. 'Come on. We're sure to find it.'

But they didn't! It had gone – for the Land of Take-What-You-Want had moved away from the Faraway Tree.

'Moon-Face! That's very bad of you!' said Joe anxiously. 'You did promise.'

Moon-Face looked worried and pale. He hunted about for the hole – but there was no hole to be seen. He began to shake with fright.

'I've g-g-g-got you all into a t-t-terrible fix!' he said, in a trembling voice. 'Here we are – stuck in a l-l-land where there's everything we w-w-want and the only thing we w-w-w-want is to get away!'

Everyone looked upset. This was just too bad!

'I feel cross with you, Moon-Face,' said Joe, in a stern voice. 'You said you'd keep guard and you didn't. I don't think you are much of a friend.'

'And I am ashamed of you too, Moon-Face,' said Silky, who had tears in her eyes.

'We'll find someone to help us,' said Moon-Face gloomily, and they all set off, followed by their hens, their goat, and the clock, which kept striking four o'clock, nobody knew why.

But now they found a very curious thing. There didn't seem to be anyone at all in the Land of Take-What-You-Want! All the gnomes, the pixies and the elves had gone.

'They must have known the land was going to move off,' said Moon-Face with a groan. 'And they all slipped down the ladder in time. Oh, why did I leave it?'

They wandered all over the land, which was not really very large, but was more crowded with things and animals than anywhere they had ever seen.

'I can't think what to *do*!' said Silky. 'It's true that there is everything here we want – we shan't starve – but it isn't the sort of place we want to live in for ever!'

They walked here and there – and then suddenly they came to something they hadn't noticed before. It was a large and shining aeroplane! The kind that was open-topped, so that you could see all round when you sat inside.

'Ooooh!' said Joe, his eyes gleaming. 'Look at that! How I wish I could fly an aeroplane! Can you fly one, Moon-Face?'

Moon-Face shook his head. Silky shook hers too. 'That's no good then,' said Joe, with a sigh. 'I thought we might fly away from this land in the airplane.'

He climbed into the aeroplane and had a good look at it. There were five handles there. One had a label on it that said 'UP'. Another had a label that said 'DOWN'. A third had one that said 'STRAIGHT ON,' and a fourth and fifth said 'TO THE RIGHT' and 'TO THE LEFT.'

Joe stared at the handles in excitement. 'I believe I could fly this aeroplane' he said. 'I do believe I could! It looks quite easy.'

'No, Joe, don't,' said Beth, in alarm. But Joe had pressed the handle labelled 'UP' and before anyone could say another word the shining aeroplane had risen upwards with Joe, leaving the others staring open-mouthed on the ground below.

'Now Joe's gone!' said Frannie, and burst into tears.

The aeroplane rose up and up. It circled round when Joe pressed the handle labelled 'TO THE RIGHT' It flew straight on when he pressed the third handle. And it flew down when he pressed the 'DOWN' handle. It was just as easy as that!

Joe flew neatly down to the ground and landed not far away from the others. They rushed to him, shouting and laughing.

'Joe! Joe! Did you really fly it yourself?'

'Well, you saw me,' said Joe, beaming at everyone and feeling tremendously proud. 'It's quite easy. Get in, everyone, and we'll fly off. Maybe we'll come to somewhere that Moon-Face knows, if we fly long enough!'

They all got in. Beth packed the seven squawking hens at the back, and sat the white goat on her knee. The shovel went on the floor. The clock made a nuisance of itself because it wouldn't stay where it was put, but kept climbing over everybody's feet to look out of the window. Silky began to wish she hadn't brought it.

'Ready?' asked Joe, pressing the handle marked 'UP'. And up they went! What a lovely feeling it was! They really couldn't help feeling excited.

Silky's clock got terribly excited too. It chimed twenty-nine without stopping.

'I shan't wind you up tonight if you don't keep quiet,' said Silky suddenly. And that finished the clock! It lay down in a corner and didn't say another ding or another dong!

'Where are we off to, I wonder?' said Beth.

But nobody knew!

XX. OFF TO DAME SNAP'S SCHOOL

Joe flew the aeroplane very well indeed. As soon as he was high enough, he pressed the 'STRAIGHT ON' handle, and the shining airplane flew forward.

The children leaned over the side to see what they were flying over. They had soon passed the Land of Take-What-You-Want, and came to a strange desolate country where no trees or grass grew, and not a house was to be seen.

'That's the Country of Loneliness,' said Moon-Face, peering over. 'Don't land there, Joe. Fly on.'

Joe flew on. Once he came to an enormous hill, and he had to quickly press the handle marked 'UP' or the aeroplane would have flown straight into it. But otherwise it really was great fun. Joe had no idea that it was so easy to fly.

The little white goat on Beth's knee was as good as gold. It licked Beth's cheek every now and then just as if it were a dog! The hens were good and quiet, and the clock lay perfectly still.

The aeroplane flew over a land of great towers and castles. 'Giantland!' said Silky, looking in wonder at the enormous buildings. 'I hope we don't land here!'

'Rather not!' said Joe, and he pressed the 'STRAIGHT ON' handle down still further, so that the aeroplane flew forward like a bird, faster and faster.

The children's hair streamed backwards, and as for Silky's mop of golden hair, it looked like a field of buttercups blown in the wind! Over the Land of Lollipop they went, and over the Country of Flop. And then the airplane began to make a funny noise!

'Hallo!' said Joe. 'What's wrong?'

'I believe the aeroplane's tired,' said Moon-Face. 'It sounds out of breath.'

'Don't be silly, Moon-Face,' said Joe. 'Airplanes don't get out of breath.'

'This kind does,' said Moon-Face. 'Can't you hear it panting?'

It certainly seemed as if the aeroplane *was* panting! 'Er-her – er-her – er-her!' it went.

'Had we better go down and give it a rest?' said Joe. 'Yes,' said Moon-Face, peering over the side. 'It seems safe enough. I don't know what land this is, but it looks quite ordinary. There's a big green house down below with an enormous garden. Perhaps you could land on that long smooth lawn, Joe. It shouldn't get too bumpy then.'

'Right,' said Joe, and pressed the handle marked 'DOWN.' And down they went, gliding smoothly. Bump! They reached the grass and ran along on the airplane's big wheels. It stopped, and everyone got out, glad to stretch their legs.

'Ten minutes' rest, and the aeroplane will be ready to go off again,' said Moon-Face, patting it.

'I wonder where we are,' said Silky, looking round. Moon-Face gazed at the big green house in the distance – and then he frowned.

'Oh my!' he groaned. 'I know whose house that is!

It's a school and it belongs to old Dame Snap! All the naughty pixies and gnomes and fairies are sent there to learn to behave better! Let's hope Dame Snap doesn't catch sight of *us*!'

Everyone looked about nervously – suddenly down a path came a tall old woman, with large spectacles on her long nose and a big white bonnet on her head. Moon-Face ran to the airplane.

'Quick!' he said. 'It's Dame Snap!'

But the old lady was up to them before they could escape. 'Aha!' she said. 'So here is another lot of naughty folk sent to me to be cured! Come this way, please.'

'We *haven't* been sent to you,' said Joe. 'We landed here to give our aeroplane a rest. We are on our way home.'

'Naughty boy, to tell stories like that!' said Dame Snap, suddenly, in such a loud and frightening voice that it made him jump. 'Come with me, all of you.'

There didn't seem to be anything else they could do. Joe, Beth, Frannie, Moon-Face, Silky, the white goat, and the seven hens followed Dame Snap, looking very miserable. The clock wouldn't walk, so Silky had to carry it.

Everyone felt very hungry. Joe pulled Dame Snap's sleeve timidly. 'Could we please have something to eat?' he asked.

'A meal will be ready in a few minutes,' said Dame Snap, 'Heads up, everyone! Don't stoop, little girl!' snapped the old woman. The little girl she meant was poor Frannie, who got such a fright that she stood up straight. Really, Dame Snap was not at all a nice person. It was very bad luck to have landed in her garden.

But everybody cheered up a little at the thought of a meal. They were taken into a large hall, full of pixies and other fairy folk. They were all sitting down in rows at wooden tables, but they stood up when Dame Snap came into the room.

'Sit over there,' said Dame Snap, pointing to an empty table. The children, Moon-Face, Silky, the goat, and the hens all took their places. The clock was stood at the end, and looked very sulky. The children looked down the tables. Oooh! What lovely cakes! What big jugs of lemonade!

Dame Snap ran her eyes over the little folk standing at the tables. She frowned. 'Twinkle, come here!' she snapped. A small pixie walked up to her.

'Haven't I told you to brush your hair properly for meal-times?' shouted Dame Snap so loudly into Twinkle's ear, that he burst into tears.

'And there's Doodle over there with a torn shirt!' said Dame Snap. 'Come here Doodle.'

Doodle came and was shouted at very loudly indeed. Beth and Frannie felt nervous, and hoped their hair and hands and dresses were clean and tidy.

'Sit!' said Dame Snap, and everyone sat. 'Have a cake?' said Joe, and passed Beth and Frannie a plate of delicious-looking cakes, with cherries in the middle.

But what a shock for them! As soon as the cakes touched their plates they turned into round hard pieces of stale bread! The children didn't dare to say a word. They saw that the same thing happened to everyone in the room except Dame Snap, who had a marvellous meal of cakes, lemonade and sandwiches.

The lemonade turned into water as soon as it was poured into the children's glasses. It was all dreadfully disappointing. In the middle of the meal a gnome-servant came in to say that someone wanted to speak to Dame Snap, and she went out of the room.

And then, dear me, the children found that the pixies and fairies in the room were really very naughty indeed! They crowded round them and jabbed at them and pinched them, and made such rude remarks that Frannie began to cry.

They made such a noise that nobody heard Dame Snap coming back again! My goodness, wasn't she angry! She clapped her hands together and made everyone jump nearly out of their skin!

'What's all this?' she snapped loudly, in a very fierce voice. 'Form up in a line! March past me at once!'

To the children's dismay the cross old lady shouted right in everyone's ear as they passed – but when *they* passed her she didn't shout at them, for she knew that they had been teased by the others. So they were very glad indeed, and felt a little more cheerful.

'Go to the schoolroom,' said Dame Snap, when the last of the line had gone by. So to the schoolroom they all went and took their places, even the little green-winged hens.

'Now, please, answer the questions written on the

blackboard,' said Dame Snap. 'You have each got paper and pencil. Anyone putting down the wrong answers will be very sorry indeed.'

Joe looked at the questions on the board. He read them out to the others, in great astonishment.

'If you take away three caterpillars from one bush, how many berries will there be left?'

'Add a pint of milk to a pound of peas and say what will be left over.'

'If a train runs at six miles an hour and has to pass under four tunnels, say what the driver's mother is likely to have for dinner on Sundays.'

Everybody gazed at the board in despair. Whatever did the questions mean? They seemed to be nonsense.

'I can't do any,' said Moon-Face, in a loud voice, and he threw down his pencil.

'It's all silly nonsense!' said Joe, and he threw down his pencil too. The girls did the same, and Silky tore her paper in half! All the pixie and fairy-folk stared at them in the greatest astonishment and horror.

'*In*deed!' said Dame Snap, suddenly looking twice as big as usual. 'If that's how you feel, come with me!'

Nobody wanted to go with her – but they found that they had to, for their legs walked them after Dame Snap without them even trying to. It was most extraordinary. Dame Snap led them to a small room and pushed them all in. Then she shut the door with a slam and turned the key in the lock.

'You will stay there for three hours, and then I will come and see if you are sorry,' she snapped.

'This is awful,' said Joe gloomily. 'She's no right to keep us here. We don't belong to her silly school. We haven't been naughty. It was just an accident that we came here.'

'Well, what are we to do now?' said Silky, pushing back her golden hair. 'It seems as if we'll have to stay here for three hours, and then say we're sorry and be shouted at again! I don't like it at all.'

Nobody liked it. They all sat on the floor and looked angry and miserable. If only they could escape from Dame Snap's silly old school!

XXI. SILKY'S CLOCK IS VERY CLEVER

Joe sat hunched up near to Moon-Face. Silky and Beth and Frannie talked together. The white goat sat on Beth's knee and slept. The seven hens tried to scratch the hard floor, and clucked softly.

'Where's my clock?' said Silky suddenly.

Everyone looked round the room for it. It wasn't there.

'It must have been left behind in the school-room,' said Joe. 'Never mind, Silky. You may get it back, if we get out of here in three hours' time.'

'I hope so,' said Silky. 'It was a nice clock, and I liked it having feet to walk about on.'

'It's lucky not to be locked up like us,' said Joe gloomily. 'If there was a window in this silly round room, we might break it and escape through that. But there isn't even a small window.'

'And there isn't a fireplace either,' said Moon-Face. 'If there was we might squeeze up the chimney. Listen!' he said suddenly. 'There's someone knocking at the door!'

They listened. Certainly there *was* someone outside, knocking gently.

'Come in, if you can!' said Moon-Face. 'Unlock the door if the key's left in.'

But the key wasn't left in! No, Dame Snap had taken that away, you may be sure!

'Who's there?' asked Silky.

'Ding-dong-ding-dong!' said a voice softly.

'It's my clock!' cried Silky excitedly. 'It's come to join us!'

'Oooh!' said Moon-Face, his big face going red with joy. 'Tell your clock to go and get the key from somewhere and let us out, Silky.'

'That's no good,' said Silky. 'I noticed that Dame Snap wore all her keys on a string that hung from her waist. The clock could never get our key from her.'

'Oh,' said Moon-Face sadly. Everybody thought hard.

'Ding-dong-ding-dong!' said the clock outside, and knocked again.

'Look here, clock, it isn't any good your dinging and donging and knocking to get in!' called Joe. 'We are locked into this room, and we haven't got a key to get us out!'

'Dong!' said the clock dolefully. And then it gave an excited 'ding!' and began to dance about on its big feet, up and down, with the little door in its back wide open.

'Whatever is that clock doing?' said Silky, in astonishment.

'Warming its feet up, I think,' said Frannie, with a giggle.

But it wasn't. For it was an old clock that had to be wound up with its own key. And it was jumping about trying to jolt its own key off the little hook inside it! At last it managed to do it. Clang! The key fell to the ground.

'What*ever* is your clock doing?' said Joe to Silky. 'It must have gone mad.'

It hadn't. It was being very sensible. It kicked at the key with one of its feet – and the key slid under the door and into the room where the children were.

'Oooh, look!' said Moon-Face, in astonishment. 'Your clock has jiggled its key off the hook – and kicked it under the door, Silky. Really, it's a most peculiar clock!'

Joe snatched up the key. 'It might fit the door!' he said. He tried it in the lock. It almost turned but not quite. He was dreadfully disappointed.

But Moon-Face grinned. He took the key and rubbed it with a little magic powder that he kept in a box in his pocket.

'Now try it,' he said. So Joe slipped it into the lock once more – and it turned right round and unlocked the door!

They crowded quietly out of the room, Joe taking the clock's key with him. Silky gave the clock a hug and it said ding-dong quite loudly with joy!

'Ssh!' said Silky. 'Don't make a sound!'

'We'll try and find our aeroplane,' said Joe. 'Let's try to get out of a door into the garden. We shall soon find it then.'

They tiptoed down a long passage – but just as they got to the end, who should they see coming along but old Dame Snap herself!

'Quick! Hide behind these curtains!' said Joe. They slipped behind them – but Dame Snap had heard something and came up to the curtains. She was going to pull them apart when Silky's clock walked out,

126

shouted 'Ding-dong!' in her ear, and trod on her toes! Dame Snap gave a shout of rage and she kicked out at the clock. But she missed and it ran away down the passage, with Dame Snap running after it.

'Good old clock!' said Silky joyfully. 'It just walked out and ding-donged in time. Another minute and we would all have been found.'

'Come on,' said Moon-Face, peeping out of the curtains. 'We'd better do our best to get into the garden now, whilst the old dame is out of the way.'

They tiptoed down a long room and came to a door leading into the garden. Just as Joe was going to open it he pushed them all quickly back into the room.

'Dame Snap is coming in here!' he whispered. 'Quick! Hide behind the furniture!'

So, quick as lightning, everyone crouched down behind the sofas and chairs, whilst Dame Snap opened the door and came in, grumbling. 'Wait till I get that clock!'

And at that very moment the clock came running in on its flat feet and ding-donged very rudely at her! Dame Snap picked up her long skirts and tore down the long room and up the passage after it! The children and Moon-Face and Silky, the hens and the goats, rushed to the garden door, opened it and crowded out into the garden.

'Find the aeroplane, quick!' cried Joe. They ran down the path and looked for the shining airplane.

'There it is!' shouted Moon-Face, pointing to the plane standing waiting on the smooth grass. They all ran to it, and squeezed in.

'I don't like leaving my clock behind,' said Silky. 'It

has been so clever. I wonder where it is.'

'Look! There it is, with old Dame Snap after it!' cried Joe. Sure enough they saw the clock come waddling out from behind a bush, chiming hard – and Dame Snap was after it, panting, and very red in the face.

The clock dodged neatly round a bush. Dame Snap tripped over a stone and fell down. The clock shot away to the aeroplane, and Silky helped it in. It sank down into a corner, and chimed sixty-three times without stopping.

But this time nobody minded. They thought the clock was really quite a hero!

Dame Snap picked herself up and ran towards the aeroplane. Joe pressed the 'UP' handle. The engine started to whirr and hum. The airplane quivered and shook. It rose gently into the air, and left Dame Snap below looking very angry indeed.

'Answer this question!' shouted Moon-Face, leaning overboard. 'If five people, seven hens, one white goat, and a clock go up in an airplane, write down how many times Dame Snap will have shouted at them by the time they get home!'

Everyone giggled.

'Do be careful where we land next time,' said Beth. 'We really must get home soon.'

'I think I know where we are now,' said Moon-Face as they flew over a curious land where the trees were yellow and the grass was pink. 'If you can fly straight on till you come to a silver tower – then fly right till you come to the Land of Seagulls – then to the left over the Three Bears' Wood – we shall soon be home!'

'Right!' said Joe. He watched out for the silver tower, and when he saw it, tall and gleaming, he pressed the handle marked 'TO THE RIGHT' and flew on till he came to the Land of Seagulls. This was quite easy to know, for all round and about, flying on snow-white wings, were hundreds of magnificent gulls. The airplane had to go slowly through the crowds of lovely birds. Joe flew to the left, and soon they were over the Three Bears' Wood, and saw the rose-covered cottage where Goldilocks lived with the bears.

'Good! Now it won't be long before we're home!' said Joe. He flew on till he came over the Enchanted Wood, and then landed in a field not far from it. Everyone jumped out.

'That was a most exciting adventure,' said Frannie. 'But I hope we never see Dame Snap again!'

'Oh quick, catch the clock!' said Beth. 'It's trying to climb out of the plane and it will fall!'

'Dong, dong, dong, dong!' said the clock, and it slid to the ground.

'We'll have to rush home now,' said Joe, picking up his shovel. 'Goodbye Silky; goodbye Moon-Face. See you soon! Beth, bring the goat, and Frannie and I will shoo the hens in front of us.'

They left the aeroplane for Moon-Face and Silky to do what they liked with, and set off home.

And, dear me, *how* astonished

their mother was to see the green-winged hens, the snow-white goat, and the fine garden shovel!

'You must have been to the Enchanted Wood,' she said.

'We've been *much* farther than that!' said Joe. And they certainly had, hadn't they?

XXII. UP TO THE LAND OF TOYS

KNOCKITY-KNOCK-KNOCK

Bang-bang-BANG!

Rat-a-tarra-TAT!

'Good gracious! It sounds as if somebody's at the door!' said Joe. 'I'll go and open it, Mother.'

He went to open the door – and outside, looking very impatient, stood the old Saucepan Man. He was hung about with pots and pans and kettles as usual, and had a saucepan for a hat.

'Hello,' said the Saucepan Man, 'didn't you hear me knock? I've come to tell you that we must go to the top of the Faraway Tree tomorrow. There's a very nice land coming there.'

'What is it?' asked Joe.

'Toyland,' said Saucepan. 'You could bring a bag with you and collect quite a lot in time for Christmas.'

'Oh what a good idea!' said Joe. He called to his two sisters. 'Beth! Frannie! Did you hear what the Saucepan Man said?'

'Yes!' they cried running to the door. 'Oh, Saucepan, we really must come. Can we help ourselves to toys, do you think?'

'Well, I've an aunt there,' said Saucepan, 'and if I tell her you're my friends, you can have what you want. Can you meet me at the top of the Faraway Tree tomorrow morning?'

'Oh, yes – and will Moon-Face and Silky be coming too?' asked Beth, happily. 'We haven't seen them for ages.'

'We'll have *fun*!' said Frannie.

'Yes, please,' said Saucepan unexpectedly. 'I'd like one very much.'

'Like what?' said Beth, astonished.

'What you just offered me – a bun,' said Saucepan, looking round for it.

'Oh – you suddenly went deaf,' said Beth. 'I just said – we'll have FUN.'

'Oh! All the same I'd like a bun,' said Saucepan.

Joe got him a bun out of the cake-tin. He went off, munching happily, his pans rattling and clanging round him. 'See you tomorrow!' he called.

The next day the three children set off to the Faraway Tree. Into the dark Enchanted Wood they went, and followed the winding path they knew so well. The trees whispered round them as they went. They always seemed to have secrets to tell one another. 'Wisha-wisha-wisha,' they whispered.

They came to the Faraway Tree in the middle of the wood. It looked even more enormous than usual. It towered up into the clouds, and the children couldn't even see the top of it. Its trunk was so big that it was quite a walk to go all the way round it!

'Great! The tree's growing blackberries today,' said Joe, picking some big ripe ones.

'Well, it shouldn't then,' said Beth.

'Blackberries

grow on bushes, not on trees. The
Faraway Tree's made a mistake!'

They began to climb the tree. A
little way up it stopped growing
blackberries and grew pine-cones!

'Not so good,' said Joe. 'We can't eat
pine-cones, Faraway Tree.'

'It's a very *exciting* tree, this,' said Frannie. 'Always
growing different things all the way up – and having
people living in it too – and a slippery-slip all the way
inside from the top to the bottom. I'm glad we live
near a tree like this. We're lucky.'

'Yes. I bet a lot of children wish they lived near it
too,' said Joe, helping Beth over a steep bit. 'My
goodness, the adventures we've had!'

'Look out – I can hear Dame Washalot's dirty water
coming down!' yelled Frannie suddenly.

And, sure enough, down came a cascade of soapy
water, running down the trunk, splashing on the
boughs, and soaking a little pixie who was sitting
nearby.

'Bother!' she said. 'And I brought an umbrella with
me, too, in case I didn't hear the water coming!'

Joe laughed. 'I should put on a swim-suit next time
and not bother about an umbrella,' he said. 'Anyway,
the sun will soon dry you!'

They went up, passing little windows in the
Faraway Tree, and came to Silky's small yellow door.
They knocked, but there was no answer.

'She's gone up to the top of the tree, I expect,' said
Joe. 'Come on – we don't want to keep the others
waiting.'

They climbed right up to Moon-Face's little door. From inside came the sound of chattering, and the noise of jangling and clanging.

'The Saucepan Man's there all right,' said Joe. 'And the others, too, I should think.' He banged on the door. Moon-Face opened it, beaming all over his big round face. 'Oh, come in,' he said. 'We're just having a snack before we go.'

'What sort of snack?' asked Beth, going in with the others. 'Pop cakes? I love those.'

'No – something Saucepan bought when he was in the Land of Surprises,' said Moon-Face. 'Well-I-Never Rolls.'

'What a peculiar name,' said Joe, looking at the dish of nice crusty little rolls. 'What do they taste of?'

'Try one,' said Moon-Face. 'And tell us!'

Joe took a roll and bit into it. 'Tastes of cheese,' he said. 'No – well I never, it tastes of ginger now. No, it doesn't – it's chocolate! And now it tastes of coconut – and it's got bits of coconut in it – no, they've gone – it's treacly now. Well I never!'

'Yes. Most peculiar, isn't it?' said Moon-Face. 'No wonder they're called Well-I-Never Rolls. You just simply never know what they'll taste of next. Every chew you have tastes of something different.'

'Jolly good,' said Joe. 'I'll have another. My – this tastes of pickled onions – no, it doesn't – it's custard – lovely!'

'Mustard,' said Saucepan in disgust. 'I'd hate one to taste of mustard.'

'I said CUSTARD,' said Joe, and then made a face. 'Oh my goodness, it *is* mustard now. Horrible!'

'Just what I said. Mustard,' said Saucepan. He bit into his. 'Ah – mint! Delicious! Why, it's mint sauce, I can taste the tiny bits of mint.'

'You'll find you've got roast lamb next,' said Silky.

Saucepan looked surprised. 'No – it isn't ham,' he said.

'I said LAMB!' shouted Silky.

'No, it's not jam,' said Saucepan. 'Well I never, it's lamb! Lamb and mint sauce – how clever! Really these rolls are remarkable.'

So they were. The six of them finished up the whole dish of them. 'I wish I'd brought heaps more,' said Saucepan, getting up. 'Well, aren't we going up to Toyland? Do hurry up.'

They were all ready. They went out of Moon-Face's little round room and climbed up the topmost branch into a cloud. They came to the little ladder that led upwards through the last bit of cloud. Toyland should be at the top!

Saucepan went first. He climbed off the top rung of the ladder, and called down to the others.

'Yes, it's here. Come on!'

Up they all went, and at last stood in Toyland. But there seemed to be no toys about at all. Saucepan pointed to a town not far off. Flags flying brightly from little houses.

'There's the Village of Toys,' he said. 'Now we'll go and find my aunt.'

They set off to the village. But when they got there, Saucepan stopped and looked puzzled.

'Dear me,' he said, 'this isn't the Land I hoped. The toys are all alive – look, isn't that a teddy bear walking about?'

'Yes,' said Beth. 'Goodness – we can't take toys like these away to play with at home! They're as big as we are!'

'I'll find my aunt,' said Saucepan, and they all walked down the village street, meeting three or four sailor dolls, a curious man who had no legs but just wobbled along, and some beautifully dressed dolls.

Saucepan's aunt was nowhere to be found. She kept a toyshop, and, of course, there was no toyshop there, because the toys lived in little houses made of coloured wooden bricks.

'Your aunt lives in the other land, you silly,' said Silky. 'This must be the Land of Toys, not Toyland.'

'Oh, well – let's enjoy ourselves, anyway,' said Saucepan. 'Here comes another wobbly man. Let's try and push him over.'

The wobbly man was astonished and annoyed when Saucepan gave him a push. He wobbled over backwards and then came forwards again, only to get another push, this time from Moon-Face.

'How dare you?' cried the wobbly man in a rage. 'That's not the way for visitors to behave! I'll report you to the Captain of the Toy Soldiers!'

He wobbled off at a remarkable speed. The three children and Silky felt a bit scared.

'You shouldn't go round pushing people, Saucepan,' said Joe. 'Not even to see them wobble. I do hope we don't get into trouble.'

Saucepan suddenly went deaf and didn't hear. He hardly ever did hear when somebody scolded him. 'Look, there's a clockwork mouse running along!' he said, pointing. 'Run, mouse, run! Meeow! MEEOW!'

The clockwork mouse was very frightened when it heard Saucepan mewing. It turned and ran off at top speed, almost bumping into a toy soldier.

'Look – there's the Captain of the Soldiers,' said Beth, afraid. 'And the Wobbly Man is with him. He's complained about us, as he said he would. We'd better run away.'

'No,' said Joe. 'We can easily explain, and Saucepan must say he's sorry.'

Up marched the toy soldier, as smart as could be. He saluted – click!

'You must come with me,' said the Captain, in a commanding voice. 'You are not toys, and should not be here. Also, your behaviour must be looked into. Follow me, quick MARCH!'

'We'd better follow,' said Joe. 'He can't do anything to us; he's only a toy, even if he *is* alive. And I must say I'd rather like to see what that toy fort is like inside."

So they all followed the toy soldier and the wobbly man. Whatever was going to happen?

XXIII. THEY GET INTO TROUBLE

The Captain took them through the village and up to the wooden fort. It was very like a toy fort that Joe had once had. It even had a wooden drawbridge that could be pulled up or let down.

It was let down for them to walk over. Toy cannons stood here and there. Joe went up to one. 'Funny old cannon!' he said. 'Look there's a knob to pull back and then let go, just like the toy cannon I had in my little fort at home.'

He pulled back the knob, let it go and then BANG! The cannon went off with a loud noise! The wobbly man was so shocked that he almost fell over, and it took a lot of wobbles for him to stand upright again.

The toys in the village below were so frightened when the cannon went BANG that they rushed out of their little houses and ran for their lives! The Captain was very angry indeed.

'Now see what you've done!' he said to Joe. 'Let off the cannon, and scared everybody! You must be mad.'

'I'm very sorry,' said Joe. 'I never thought the cannon would go off like that.'

'Well, what did you think it would do?' said the Captain, angrily. 'Whistle a tune or dance a jig?'

Nobody dared to laugh. The Captain led them on again, and soon they came to a door that led into a wooden tower. They went in and found themselves in

138

a room with a table and a chair at one end, and nothing else. The Captain sat himself down in the chair.

'Stand up straight,' he said. Everyone stood up very straight, even Saucepan.

'Salute,' said the Captain, and everyone saluted, though Moon-Face used the wrong hand.

'Dismiss!' said the Captain, and everyone stared. What did he mean?

'No – that's wrong,' said the Captain. 'Don't dismiss. Stand at ease.'

They obeyed. The Captain rapped loudly on the table. 'You are accused of not being toys. You are accused of punching wobbly men. You are accused of setting off cannons. You –'

'Only *one* wobbly man, and *one* cannon,' said Joe. 'We're sorry and we won't do it again. We'll dismiss now!'

But before they could go they heard the noise of marching feet, and into the room came about fifty toy soldiers, all very wooden. They surrounded the children and the others.

'To the deepest dungeon with them!' shouted the Captain.

'NO!' shouted Joe, and he pushed the nearest soldier hard. The soldier fell against the soldier next to him and knocked him over. That one fell against the next one and he went down, too, knocking the soldier next to him – and before five seconds had passed every soldier was lying flat on the floor.

'It's like playing dominoes – knock the first over, and down goes the whole row!' said Frannie with a giggle.

The Captain looked alarmed. What was he to do with people like these? Goodness – one push, and all his soldiers were down! He banged on the table.

'Order! Order! Get up! Do you think you are skittles, men?'

The men got up, but none of them would go near the little group of six prisoners.

'Now listen,' said the Captain. 'Either you become toys, or you go to the deepest dungeon. You can choose.'

'All right – we'll be toys, then!' said Joe with a grin. 'I'll be a clockwork clown, and go head-over-heels all the time!'

He began to go head-over-heels all round the room, and knocked into one of the soldiers. Down they all went again, like a row of skittles!

'Right – you're a clockwork clown,' said the Captain. 'What will *you* be?' and he pointed at Moon-Face.

'A teddy bear,' grinned Moon-Face, 'with a growl in my middle.' And he pressed himself in the middle and pretended to growl.

'I'll be a doll,' said Silky, and began to walk about stiffly like a doll.

'And I'll be a furry grey rabbit!' said the Saucepan Man. 'I'll grow long floppy ears and grey fur!'

'We'll be dolls,' said Beth and Frannie together, and they walked about stiffly like Silky, giggling all the time.

'Right,' said the Captain thankfully. 'You are now toys, and can remain in the Land of Toys. Dis-MISS!'

The six of them went out laughing, Joe still turning

head-over-heels, just for fun. They went over the drawbridge and into the town. In the distance they saw an enormous Noah's Ark.

'Let's go and see the animals coming out two by two,' said Beth, and they set off.

Frannie was just going to say something to Saucepan, who was in front of her, when she stopped. She stared hard.

She saw something very peculiar. Saucepan wore a saucepan for a hat, as usual – but, goodness, he had suddenly grown two huge floppy ears! The saucepan sat on top, looking very odd.

'Saucepan,' said Frannie, astonished. 'Saucepan, what's wrong with you?'

Saucepan turned round, surprised, and everyone got a tremendous shock. His face was covered in grey fur and he had very long whiskers!

'He's a toy rabbit!' said Frannie, with a squeal. 'Saucepan – you're a toy rabbit! You said you would be, and now you are.'

They were all very surprised. They stared and stared at poor Saucepan. How peculiar to see his face all grey, topped with two floppy ears and long quivering whiskers!

Saucepan looked at himself in one of his bright pans, which he used as a mirror. He was shocked to see such a furry face looking back at him. He gazed round at the others, scared.

Then he gave a shout and pointed to Joe. 'Well! Look at *him*! He's a clockwork clown now, hat and all! Yes, and he's got a key in his back! Joe, you're a clown! No wonder you keep going head-over-heels!'

Joe turned another somersault at once. The others gazed at him. Yes, Joe was a clown, with a clown's hat and suit. His face was daubed in red and white like a clown's too.

Frannie looked at the others, and squealed again. 'Look at Moon-Face – he's a fat, round little teddy bear, with a round, teddy-bear face that's hardly like Moon-Face's at all! Oh, Moon-Face – is it really you?'

'Yes,' said Moon-Face, putting up his hand to feel his face. 'Oh dear – I've gone all furry. Where are my clothes? They've gone.'

Joe pressed him in the middle and an alarming growl came out – grrrrrrrrrr!

'Don't,' said Silky. 'You made me jump. Don't press him again, Joe. Oh, my goodness – this is dreadful. We're all toys. Look at *me*!'

'You're not so bad,' said Joe, looking at her. 'You are the prettiest doll I ever saw. And Beth and Frannie are dolls, too. Look at them walking about, as stiff as can be. Beth, can you sit down?'

'Not very easily,' said Beth, trying to sit on a nearby wall. 'I can't seem to bend. And I can't shut my eyes, either.'

'Perhaps they will shut when you lie down,' said Moon-Face, speaking in a funny growly voice.

So Beth lay down on some grass for a moment and at once her eyes shut!

'Yes, we're *really* toys,' said Frannie. 'It must have begun to happen when we said we'd be toys, and chose what we'd be. But we only said it for fun.'

'I know. But you never know what will happen in the Lands that come to the top of the Faraway Tree,' said Joe. 'Moon-Face, will we stop being toys when we get out of this Land?'

'No, I don't think so,' said the teddy bear. 'And anyway, how do you think you are going to head-over-heels down the Faraway Tree? We'll just have to hope this will all wear off.'

'I don't like being a toy rabbit,' said Saucepan sadly. 'I feel silly. Do you think my face will become my own again if I wash it?'

'No,' said Joe, turning head-over-heels for about the fiftieth time; 'toy rabbits always stay furry. It's your ears that look so funny with that saucepan stuck on top of them. Why don't you take it off?'

'Well, I might get a cold,' said Saucepan. 'I always wear a hat. I don't feel right without a saucepan for a hat.'

'You certainly don't *look* right now,' said Moon-Face, in his growly voice.

'Nor do you,' said Saucepan. 'I wish you'd look like Moon-Face again. I don't like you like that.'

'Oh, come on,' said Joe, going head-over-heels again. 'Let's explore the Village of Toys and hope all this wears off. If only I didn't have to go head-over-heels so often! I'm getting very tired of it.'

'So are we,' said Frannie, getting out of his way. 'Do keep over there, Joe – you'll knock me over.'

The little group went on through the Village of Toys. Nobody took much notice of them now because they looked exactly like toys. Wobbly men wobbled about, looking very busy, and teddy bears lazed around, fat and cheerful looking. Dolls of all kinds went here and there, and they saw the little clockwork mouse again.

'Meeow!' said Saucepan, and it fled.

'You're unkind to it,' said Frannie. 'It's a dear little thing. Oh, dear – I do feel funny, walking stiffly like this. I'm sure I couldn't run, even if I had to!'

'Look, here come the Noah's Ark animals,' said Joe, getting up from another somersault. 'Two by two, just as they should. Two lions, two bears, two rabbits . . .'

'Two ducks, two mice,' went on Frannie.

'MEEOW!' said Saucepan at once again. 'Meeow!'

But the Noah's Ark mice took no notice of him. However, somebody else did! Behind the mice were two cats, and one of them left the row of animals and came over to Saucepan, glaring at him.

'What did you say just then?' said the wooden cat.

'Meow,' said Saucepan, 'meow, meow, meow!'

'How dare you call me such rude names!' said the cat, and showed claws in her wooden paws. Saucepan backed away hurriedly.

'I didn't mean to call you names,' he said. 'I just said, "meow, meow, meow," to the mice.'

'Well, that means, "You're a very ugly cat with a crooked tail!"' said the cat angrily. 'My tail is *not* crooked. Don't use cat-language if you don't know what it means!'

'Get back into line, cat!' called Mr Noah, and the cat obeyed. Saucepan was very relieved. Goodness – to think those simple meows had meant all that in cat-language! He really must be careful.

'Let's go on,' he said to the others, who were as surprised as he was. 'Moon-Face might suddenly begin to growl, and goodness knows what that might mean in bear-language! We don't want those two

144

white bears and the two brown ones to come after us.'

'Well, let's go another way,' said Joe, gloomily turning another somersault. 'Blow this head-over-heels business. I'm tired of it!'

They turned down another way. Oh, dear – was this strange spell wearing off yet? It didn't seem like it!

XXIV. MR OOM-BOOM-BOOM

They came to a little garage. A very furry rabbit was busy putting petrol into a car driven by another toy rabbit. They looked at Saucepan in surprise as he came along with the others.

'Hello!' said the garage rabbit. 'What's the idea of wearing a saucepan for a hat? I can't say I've ever seen a rabbit wearing a hat before.'

'Well, you've seen one now,' said Saucepan, not very politely. 'Bother these awful floppy ears. I hate them. They make me look like a toy rabbit.'

'Well, you *are* a toy rabbit, floppy ears and all,' said the rabbit, staring.

'That's where you're wrong,' said Saucepan. 'I'm not. I hate being one. Ugly creatures, with stupid long ears and quivering whiskers!'

'Stop it, Saucepan,' said Joe, in a warning voice. He turned to the surprised rabbit.

'You must excuse him,' he said, 'he's really a Saucepan Man, as you can see. And I'm not really a clockwork clown, I'm a boy. Oh – excuse me, I can feel another somersault coming on!'

He turned head-over-heels and then stood up straight again.

'I see,' said the rabbit. 'Well, I should just hate to be an ugly little Saucepan Man, so I know what he feels about being a rabbit – though rabbits are very handsome creatures – like myself. He should be pleased he's turned into one.'

'Well, we really like being ourselves best,' said Frannie. 'I'm a little girl, not a doll. And this teddy bear is really Moon-Face.'

'Never heard of him,' said the rabbit. 'Didn't know there were such things as Moon-Faces.'

Frannie giggled. Silky went up to the rabbit and smiled at him. 'Please do help us,' she said.

The rabbit stared at her. He thought she was the prettiest doll he had ever seen in the Village of Toys. The rabbit who was inside the car leaned out.

'Of course we'll help you,' he said. 'What do you want us to do?'

'Well, we did hope all this would wear off,' said Silky in a high doll's voice that was quite sweet. 'But it hasn't. And we wondered if you knew how we could get back into ourselves again.'

The two rabbits looked at one another. 'Difficult,' said one. 'Very,' said the other.

'What about the old Spell-Maker, Mr Oom-Boom-Boom?' said the first one. 'If he's in a good mood, he might do something for them.'

'Yes. But if he's in a bad mood, he might turn them into something worse,' said the second rabbit.

'Then we won't go there,' said Joe hurriedly, and turned another somersault.

'We could see if he's in a good or bad mood before we say anything,' said the rabbit. 'I'll take you there in my car, if you can all squeeze in.'

'Well, we could try,' said Moon-Face,

147

his little round teddy bear face looking worried.

The rabbit told Silky to sit next to him. He thought she was really beautiful, and very sweet. 'I am sure, if *you* went to ask Mr Oom-Boom-Boom a favour he would say "yes" at once,' he said. 'I never saw anyone as pretty as you.'

'Well you're a very handsome rabbit,' said Silky, and that pleased him very much. They all squeezed into the car somehow, waved to the friendly garage rabbit, and set off.

'I feel a somersault coming on,' said Joe suddenly. 'I'm so sorry – but will you please stop the car so that I can get out and turn head-over-heels?'

'You're going to be a bit of a nuisance,' said the rabbit driver. 'Can't you do about a dozen, and make those do for a while?'

'I'll try,' said poor Joe. So he got out and did nine, but no more would come, so he got back into the car. 'I do wish you didn't wear so many pans and kettles,' he said to Saucepan. 'Move that kettle, will you? It's sticking its spout into me.'

'Kettles don't have snouts,' said Saucepan.

'SPOUT, I said, not Snout,' said Joe crossly. 'Now there's something else sticking into me – a saucepan handle.'

'I haven't got any candles,' said Saucepan, mishearing again. 'You know I haven't. You're just making a fuss, with all your chatter about snouts and candles.'

'I said SHOUTS and PANDLES,' bawled Joe, losing his temper. 'No, I don't mean that – I mean, I mean . . .'

'Pouts and Scandles,' said Frannie with a squeal of

laughter. 'Be quiet, you two. Saucepan, dear, be sensible. He meant Spouts and Handles – look, they're sticking into him.'

'Well, why didn't he say so then,' grumbled Saucepan, moving the kettle and the saucepan and sticking them into Moon-Face instead. 'Goodness, Moon-Face, what are *you* growling about now?'

Moon-Face turned his teddy-bear face to Saucepan. 'You're not kind,' he said.

'No, I don't mind,' said Saucepan, whose hearing had gone quite wrong with the noise of the car and the jangling of his pans. 'Of course I don't mind. Why should I mind? Mind what, anyhow?'

'Stop talking,' said the rabbit at the wheel. 'I keep listening and it all sounds so mad that I'm sure I shall drive into a tree or something. Anyway, I want to talk to this dear doll here, Silky.'

Nobody talked after that except Silky and the toy rabbit. The car went on and on, and at last Joe wanted to get out and go head-over-heels again. 'Can you stop?' he called.

'Goodness, I've gone right past Mr Oom-Boom-Boom!' said the rabbit, putting on the brake so suddenly that the saucepan flew off Saucepan's head and rolled away down the road. 'Yes, get out and somersault for a bit while I turn the car round.'

So Joe turned about ten somersaults, while the toy rabbit turned the car round again. Then back they went to find Mr Oom-Boom-Boom.

'Don't start talking to Silky or you'll go right past again,' begged Frannie. But this time the rabbit kept an eye open for Mr Oom-Boom-Boom's house and

suddenly put on the brakes again.

'There goes another of my saucepans,' groaned Saucepan. 'Do we *have* to stop so suddenly?'

Nobody took any notice of him. They stared at a funny little door set in a grassy hill. On it was printed in bold black letters:

OOM-BOOM-BOOM. KNOCK SEVEN TIMES.

'Silky, you go,' said Frannie. 'Perhaps Oom-Boom-Boom will be nice to you. You really do look very sweet.'

'All right. I'll knock,' said Silky bravely, though she felt very scared. She got out of the car, and went up to the little door. She took hold of the knocker and knocked seven times – blam-blam-blam-blam-blam-blam-blam!

A loud voice came from inside. 'Stop knocking. Once is quite enough!'

'Oh dear – he's in a bad mood!' called the rabbit. 'Come back quickly, Silky, and we'll drive off.'

'I can't come,' wailed Silky. 'The knocker has got hold of my hand. It won't let go!'

Joe jumped out at once and went to help her. But Silky was quite right. The knocker had tight hold of her hand and wouldn't let it go.

Moon-Face went to help, too, and then the Saucepan Man, looking very worried. And just at that very moment the door opened, pulling poor Silky with it, and a voice boomed out loudly:

'WHAT'S ALL THIS? DISTURBING ME IN THE MIDDLE OF MY SPELLS!'

Everyone thought that Oom-Boom-Boom was a very good name for him, booming at them like that. But he wasn't a bit like his voice. He was an old pixie with a beard so long that it trailed behind him. He had big, pointed ears, and wore a funny little round hat with feelers on it like a butterfly's. His eyes were as green as grass and very bright indeed.

He frowned at them all – and then he saw Silky, still held by the knocker.

'Ah,' he said, and a smile broke over his face like the sun shining out suddenly. 'Ah! What a dear little doll! No wonder my knocker wouldn't let you go. Where did you come from? I've never seen a doll as pretty as you! Do you know where you ought to be?'

'No,' said Silky, with a gasp.

'You ought to be standing at the very top of the great big Christmas Tree that Santa Claus has in his castle!' said Oom-Boom-Boom in his booming voice. 'He's always looking for the prettiest doll in the world to put there, but he's never found one as pretty as you yet!'

'I'm not a doll,' said Silky. 'I'm a fairy. I've been turned into a doll today.'

'Let her go, knocker,' said the pixie. 'Come in, all of you. Why have you paid me this visit?'

'He seems in a very good mood now,' whispered Joe to Moon-Face. 'I think it's safe to go in.'

They all went in and the door shut with a bang that

151

made them jump. Inside there was a narrow, very winding passage that led into the hill. They followed the pixie down it, everybody stumbling over his very long beard that trailed out behind him. He didn't seem to mind.

He took them to a big room with a very low ceiling. A great fire burned in the middle, but the flames were green, not red, and no heat came from them.

'I was just making a few spells,' said Oom-Boom-Boom, his big voice echoing all round the room. 'I'm a spell-maker, you know.'

'Yes. That's why we came,' said Silky, feeling very nervous. 'Please, dear Mr Oom-Boom-Boom, will you use a spell to help us? We want to go back to our right selves. I'm a fairy, really, as I told you.'

'And we're really little girls,' said Beth and Frannie. 'And this clown is a boy, and the toy rabbit is old Saucepan Man...'

'And I'm Moon-Face,' said Moon-Face, his little teddy-bear face looking very earnest. 'Please do help us.'

'Ha,' said Oom-Boom-Boom, looking round at them and beaming, 'well, I don't mind doing that. That's easy. But I'll do it on one condition.'

'What's that?' asked Joe, his heart sinking.

'I'll turn five of you back to your own shapes – but I want this little doll here, the very pretty one, to stay with me so that I can sell her to Santa Claus to put on the top of his Christmas Tree! It will be such an honour for her. You'd love that, wouldn't you, my dear?' he said to Silky, turning to her.

Silky looked very frightened. 'Well – I'll stay and let

you sell me to Santa Claus,' she said, 'if you will use a spell on the others.'

'Oh, dear, darling Silky!' said Moon-Face, putting his furry arm round her, 'How sweet you are! But we wouldn't let you. We'd never leave you here alone.'

'Never,' said Joe. 'NEVER!'

'Never, never, never, never,' said Joe, Beth and Frannie.

'I'm going to stay,' said Silky, looking as if she was going to cry, but smiling at them all the same. 'It won't be so bad, going to Santa Claus, though it sounds very dull standing on the top of his Christmas Tree. But it's for you, you see, so I want to do it!'

'Of course she wants to do it,' said Oom-Boom-Boom. 'She's a sensible little doll.'

'Be quiet,' said Joe. 'I tell you we won't let her do it! We'd rather be toys all our lives than that!'

Then Mr Oom-Boom-Boom lost his temper. He rushed at Joe – but Joe did a very clever thing. He caught him by his very long beard, dragged him to a big table and tied him to it with his beard, making dozens of knots!

'Now, quick, let's go!' he cried. 'Sorry about tying you up, Oom-Boom-Boom, but you're not going to have Silky. Run everyone!'

They ran up the winding passage and came out on the hillside. And oh, thank goodness, there was the rabbit waiting in his car! What a wonderful sight!

XXV. IN SANTA CLAUS' CASTLE

Joe got to the car first. 'Quick!' he cried. 'I can hear Oom-Boom-Boom coming! He must have got free.'

So he had! He appeared at the door of his peculiar house, and they saw that he had freed himself by cutting his beard short. He did look strange.

The toy rabbit revved up his car and it shot off, almost before Saucepan was safely in. A kettle flew, clanging, down the road, and Saucepan groaned.

'Well, thank goodness that kettle's gone,' said Joe. 'It can't stick into me again. Oh, dear – I feel I want to turn head-over-heels.'

'Well, you can't,' said Moon-Face firmly. 'Unless you want to be caught by the Oom-Boom-Boom fellow. Here, Saucepan, hang on to Joe, and stop him turning head-over-heels in the car!'

It was difficult to stop him, but they managed it. After they had gone a good way the rabbit stopped the car for a talk, and Joe took the chance of turning about a dozen somersaults.

'You know, I think you should go to the Land of Santa Claus,' said the rabbit. 'I do really. Not to give him Silky, of course, that would never do – but to tell him you aren't toys and to ask him if he can stop you being what you're not.'

'That's a bit muddling,' said Moon-Face, trying to work it out. 'Yes – it seems a good idea. After all, he deals in toys, doesn't he? He must know them very well. He'll be able to tell we're not real toys, and *might* help us.'

'We know he's kind,' said Silky. 'He's so fond of children. Let's go to him. How can we get there, though? This Land may stay at the top of the Faraway Tree for some time – and the Land of Santa Claus may not be the next one to arrive.'

'That's true enough,' said the rabbit. 'Actually the next Land on the timetable is the Land of Squalls, which doesn't sound too good. But I'll tell you what I can do for you!'

'What!' asked Joe.

'I can drive you to the next station and put you on a train for the Land of Santa Claus,' said the toy rabbit. 'I happened to notice that some trains there do go to his Land. What about it, friends?'

'A very good idea,' said everyone, and off they went. They came to a funny little station after a while, and they all got out.

'I wish you could stay in my Land for ever, Silky doll,' said the rabbit to Silky. 'You really are the prettiest thing I ever saw. But there – you'd be unhappy and I couldn't bear that.'

'I'll write to you,' said Silky.

'Will you really?' said the rabbit. 'Do you know, I've never had a letter in my life! It *would* make me feel important! Look, there's a train in!'

'Wow! This train's going to the Land of Santa Claus! What a bit of luck!' cried Moon-Face. 'Goodbye, rabbit. You really have been a good friend. I'll write to you.'

'My goodness – fancy me getting two letters!' said the delighted rabbit.

'We'll *all* write,' said Joe, shaking his furry hand warmly. 'Goodbye. It's been lovely meeting you.'

Silky gave him a kiss and he nearly cried for joy. 'I've never been kissed before,' he said. 'Never. A kiss – and letters – my goodness, I *am* a lucky rabbit!'

They all climbed into the train and waved goodbye.

'Nice fellow, that rabbit,' said Joe. 'Well, we're off again. I wonder how far it is.'

It was quite a long way, and they all fell asleep. A porter woke them up at last. 'Hey, you! Don't you want to get out here?' he said. 'This is where toys usually get out.'

They scrambled out because the station board said, 'Get out here for the Castle of Santa Claus!'

'Just in time,' said Joe, yawning. 'Oh – here I go, turning head-over-heels again!'

'There's the castle – look!' said Beth, pointing to a magnificent castle with many towers, rising high on a hill nearby. 'And, goodness – look at the snow!

Anyone would think it was winter here.'

'Oh, it always is,' said the porter. 'It wouldn't be much good for sleighs, would it, if there wasn't snow? Is Santa Clause expecting you? His sleigh usually meets the train in case there are any visitors for him.'

'Is that it down there?' asked Moon-Face, pointing down into the snowy station yard. A sleigh was there, with four lovely reindeer, whose bells jingled as they moved restlessly. A small red pixie held the reins.

'Yes, that's the sleigh. Better go and get in,' said the porter. He stared hard at Silky. 'Goodness, isn't that a pretty doll? I bet Santa Claus will want her for his own Christmas Tree.'

They went to the sleigh and got into it. 'To Santa Claus, please,' said Joe, and off they went, gliding smoothly over the snow, drawn by the four eager reindeer.

They arrived at the castle. They felt rather nervous when they saw how big and grand it was. They stood at an enormous door, carved with all kinds of toys, and rang a great bell.

The door swung open. 'Please come in,' said a teddy bear, dressed like a footman. 'Santa Claus will see you in a few minutes.'

They went into a big hall and then into a great room, where many little pixies and goblins were at work. 'You might like to look round while you're waiting,' said the bear footman. 'You'll see the pixies painting the dolls' houses, and the goblins putting growls into us bears, and you'll see how the somersaults are put into the clockwork clowns.'

'I don't want to see that,' said Joe, feeling at once

that he wanted to go head-over-heels. He turned a few and then stood up again. 'What are those pixies doing over there?' he said.

'Putting the hum into tops,' said the footman. 'But don't go too near. One of the hums might get into you by mistake, and that's *such* a nuisance, you know!'

They stood at a safe distance, watching. It was very interesting indeed. So many things were going on; there was so much to see and hear, that they almost forgot they were toys themselves.

'How's your growl, bear?' said a little pixie, running up to Moon-Face. He pressed him in the middle and Moon-Face growled deeply. 'Grrrrrr! Leave me alone! I don't like people doing that. Grrrrr!'

'Look – oh, look – isn't that Santa Claus himself?' cried Beth, suddenly, as a big man came into the room dressed in bright red. He wore a hood trimmed with white, and his jolly face had eyes that twinkled brightly.

'Yes. It's Santa Claus!' cried Joe. Santa Claus heard him and came over at once. He looked in surprise at Silky.

'Why!' he said, 'where did you come from? *You* weren't made in my castle, by pixies and goblins. You are the loveliest doll I've ever seen. I've a good mind to keep you for myself and put you at the very top of my own big Christmas Tree.'

'No, no, please not!' said Silky. Santa Claus looked down at the others. He seemed puzzled.

'Where do you all come from?' he said. 'I am quite sure I have never had any toys made like you. The rabbit, dressed up in kettles and saucepans, for instance – and this funny little bear. He doesn't seem like a proper teddy.'

'We're *not* proper toys!' said Beth. 'Santa Claus, we got turned into toys in the fort of the toy soldiers. I'm a little girl really.'

'And I'm Moon-Face, who lives at the top of the Faraway Tree,' said Moon-Face.

'What! The famous Moon-Face, who has a slippery-slip in his room, going down the tree from the top to the bottom!' cried Santa Claus. 'My goodness – I've often wanted to see that! Do you think I'm too fat to go down it?'

'No – no, I don't think so,' said Moon-Face, looking at him. 'I could give you *two* cushions to sit on instead of one. If you'd like to come now, you can go up and down the Faraway Tree as often as you like – we'll haul you up in the washing basket every time you arrive at the bottom, and you can slide down again from the top!'

'Let's go now,' said Santa Claus in delight. 'Well, well – to think I'm meeting the famous Moon-Face at last! And I suppose this lovely doll is Silky the fairy. And, of course – this is the old Saucepan Man!'

'But – how do you know us?' asked Moon-Face, astonished.

'Oh, I've heard about you from the children,' said Santa Claus. 'They keep asking me for books about you, to go into their Christmas stockings and they looked so exciting that I read them all. I *did* want to meet you!'

Well, wasn't that a bit of luck? Santa Claus called his sleigh and they all got in. 'To the top of the

Faraway Tree,' commanded Santa Claus, and away they went. It didn't take very long. In quite a little while the sleigh landed on a broad bough near the top of the tree, and they all got out.

'My room is just a bit higher up,' said Moon-Face, and led the way. They were soon in his little round room. He pointed to the curious hole in the middle of the floor.

'There you are,' he said. 'That's the slippery-slip – it goes round and round from top to bottom of the tree – and you fly out of the trap door at the bottom, and land on a soft cushion of moss.'

'Splendid!' said Santa Claus. 'Will somebody else go first, please? Goodness, it's exactly the same as I read about in the books!'

'Er – do you think you could just change us back to our ordinary selves?' asked Joe, afraid that in his excitement Santa Claus might forget to do what they so badly wanted. 'I feel as if I'm going to somersault again, and I don't want to turn head-over-heels all the way down the slippery-slip.'

'Change you back? Yes, of course; it's easy!' said Santa Claus. 'The slippery-slip is just the right place for a spell. Shut your eyes, please.'

They all shut their eyes. Santa Claus touched each

one gently, chanting a curious little song:

'Go in as you are,
Come out as you were,
Go in as you are,
Come out as you were!'

They opened their eyes. Moon-Face got a cushion and pulled Beth on to it. He gave her a tremendous push and she shot down the slippery-slip at top speed – round and round – and then out she flew through the trap door at the bottom, and landed on a tuft of moss.

'Oh,' she said, breathless. 'Oh! I'm myself again. I'm not a stiff-jointed doll any longer – and I can shut and open my eyes properly!'

She got up – and out of the trap door flew Joe. 'Joe! You're all right again! You're you!' cried Beth in delight. 'And here comes Silky – she's not a doll any more – and here's Frannie – she's all right, too. Look out – here's the old Saucepan Man – yippee he's back to normal!'

'And he's lost his floppy ears,' said Silky. 'I'm rather sorry. I liked him with those long ears. Good old Saucepan.'

And then, WhoooooOOOOOOSH! The trap door shot open with a bang and out sailed Santa Claus, his hood on the back of his head! Bump! He went on to the cushion of moss, and sat there, panting and full of delight.

'What a thrill! WHAT a thrill! Better than anything I've got in my castle.'

'Look out! Here comes Moon-Face!' cried Joe, and out came Moon-Face, no longer a fat teddy bear, but his own beaming self once more.

'I'd like to do that again,' said Santa Claus, standing up. 'How did you say we got back to the top of the tree? In a basket?'

'Yes,' said Joe, 'but if you don't mind, we won't come with the others. You see, our mother will be wondering about us. So we'd better say goodbye and thank you very much.'

'Goodbye. See you next Christmas,' said Santa Claus. 'I'll bring you something extra nice. Ah – here comes the basket, let down on a rope. Do we get in?'

The last thing that Joe, Beth and Frannie saw was Santa Claus in the big basket, being pulled slowly up by all the squirrels at the top of the tree. Moon-Face and Silky and Saucepan were with him, leaning over the edge of the basket, waving to them.

'Well – I suppose dear old Santa Claus will be going down that slippery-slip till it's dark,' said Joe. 'Oh dear – surely I'm not going to turn head-over-heels again! I feel just like it!'

'Oh, you'll soon get out of the habit,' said Beth. 'I still feel as if I want to walk stiffly like a doll. Goodness, wasn't that an adventure!'

'We'll never have a better one,' said Frannie.

Oh yes, you will, Frannie, Beth and Joe. You just wait and see!

XXVI. THE ARMY OF RED GOBLINS

One day Mother said that since she had to be out for
the whole day, she would prefer if the children asked
the Old Saucepan Man to come and stay with them,
and bring any other two friends they had made.

'Good!' said Joe. 'We'll ask Moon-Face and Silky.'

Beth wrote a note, and gave it to the little white
goat to take to Moon-Face.

The white goat was a wonderful creature. It gave
the most delicious milk, it ran errands, and if any of
the hens got out, it found them and drove them back.
It was most useful.

The goat took the note in its mouth, and ran off to
the Enchanted Wood. It came to the Faraway Tree
and bleated to the red squirrel, who peeped out from
his hole low down in the trunk.

The squirrel took the note and bounded up to
Moon-Face with it. Moon-Face was delighted, and
shouted down to Silky, who came up and read it.

'We'll ask the Old Saucepan Man as soon as Mister
Watzisname is asleep,' said Moon-Face. 'The children
haven't asked Watzisname – so Saucepan will have to
creep down the tree with us, without telling him.'

They sent a note back by the little goat, saying that
they would arrive at three o'clock that afternoon. The
children were excited. Mother was preparing to leave,
and the girls began to make the cottage look pretty

164

with jars of flowers. Beth baked some chocolate cakes, and Frannie made some toffee. Joe made up some sandwiches.

'We'll have a wonderful time,' he said. 'I hope the Saucepan Man won't be too deaf this afternoon.'

By three o'clock everything was ready. The children were neat and clean. The table looked fine with its sandwiches, cakes, and toffee. Beth went to the gate to look for their visitors.

She couldn't see them coming down the lane. 'They *are* late!' she called to the others. 'I expect the Saucepan Man has got tangled up with his saucepans or something!'

Half-past three came and no visitors. The children were rather disappointed. 'Perhaps Moon-Face read my letter wrongly, and thought it was four o'clock,' said Beth.

But when four o'clock came and still no Moon-Face, Silky or Saucepan Man arrived, they got really worried.

'I do hope nothing has happened,' said Beth, feeling upset. 'There's all our nice food and nobody to eat it.'

'We'll wait a bit longer, then we'll eat our share,' said Joe. So, when five o'clock came, and nobody had arrived, the children sadly ate half of the food themselves.

'Something's happened,' said Joe gloomily.

'Oh dear! What do you think it is?' said Beth, alarmed. 'Could we go and see?'

'No,' said Joe. 'Not now, anyway. Mother will be back soon. We'd better go tonight. The rope is let down the

165

Tree then for us to pull ourselves up, and it won't take long to climb up.'

'We really must find out what's wrong,' said Beth, clearing the plates away. 'We'll take their share of the food with us.'

So, that night, when it was quite dark, the three children slipped out of bed, dressed, and crept out of the back door. They took a lantern that Joe had found, for there was no moon that night. Joe swung it in front of him and they could see where to walk.

Down the dark lane they went, over the ditch and into the Enchanted Wood. The trees were whispering very loudly together tonight. 'Wisha-wisha-wisha!' they said.

'Oh, how I wish I knew what they were saying!' said Frannie.

'Come on,' said Joe. 'We'd better not be too long, Frannie. We want to be back by daylight.'

They made their way through the dark wood. As there was no moon there were no fairy-folk about at all that night. The children soon came to the Faraway Tree, and looked for the rope.

But there was no rope at all this time – and they had to begin to climb up as usual, holding onto the boughs and branches carefully, for it was very difficult to see.

Before they had got farther than two branches up, a strange thing happened. Someone caught hold of Joe's shoulder and pushed him roughly down! Joe fell, caught hold of the lowest branch, and just saved himself in time.

'Who did that?' he cried angrily. He undid his

lantern from his belt, where he had put it whilst climbing, and flashed it up the Tree, calling to Beth and Frannie to go no farther.

And standing grinning in the lower branches of the tree were four red goblins, with pointed ears, wide mouths, and wicked little eyes!

'No one is allowed to come up the Tree now,' said one of the goblins. 'And no one is allowed to come down either.'

'But why not?' asked Joe, astonished.

'Because it's *our* Tree now!'

'*Your* Tree! What nonsense!' said Joe. 'We've come to see our friends who live in the Tree. Let us pass.'

'No!' said the goblins, and they grinned widely. 'You – can't – come – up!'

'It's no good,' said a tiny voice beside Joe. 'The goblins have taken everyone prisoner in the tree. If you go up they'll only push you down, or take you prisoners too.'

Joe flashed his lantern downwards, and the children saw that it was the little red squirrel speaking – the one who looked after the cushions for Moon-Face.

'Hallo!' said Joe. 'Do tell me what's happened. I can't understand it!'

'Oh, it's easy enough to understand,' said the squirrel. 'The Land of the Red Goblins came to the top of the Faraway Tree. The goblins found a hole that leads down through the clouds, and poured down it! They took everyone prisoner. Moon-Face and everyone else are locked up in their houses in the tree-trunk. I can tell you Mister Watzisname and the Angry Pixie have nearly battered their doors down in rage!'

167

'But why have the goblins locked them up?' asked Beth, in surprise.

'Well, they want some magic spells that the Tree-dwellers know,' said the squirrel. 'They are going to keep them all locked up till they tell the spells. Isn't it dreadful?'

'Oh dear!' said Frannie. 'Whatever can we do to help them?'

'I don't know,' said the squirrel sadly. 'If only you could get up to them you might be able to make some plan. But the goblins won't let anyone up the Tree.'

'Wisha-wisha-wisha-wisha!' whispered the trees loudly.

'You know, I can't help feeling that the trees want to tell us something tonight,' said Beth suddenly. 'I always feel that they are whispering secrets to one another – but tonight I feel that they want to tell them to *us*!'

'I shouldn't be surprised,' said the squirrel. 'The Faraway Tree is King of the Wood, and now that trouble has come to it all the other trees are angry. Perhaps they want to help us.'

'Wisha-wisha-wisha-wisha,' said the trees loudly.

'Put your arms round a tree-trunk and press your left ear to the tree,' said the squirrel suddenly. 'I have heard it said that that is the only way to hear a tree's words.'

Each of the children found a small tree. They put their arms round the trunks and pressed their left ears

168

to the trees. And then they could quite clearly hear what the trees were whispering.

'Help the Faraway Tree-dwellers!' the leaves whispered. 'Help them!'

'But how can we?' whispered back the children eagerly. 'Tell us!'

'Go up the slippery-slip,' said the trees, in their leafy voices. 'Go through the trap-door and up the slippery-slip!'

'Oh!' cried the children all at once. 'Of course! Why ever didn't we think of it ourselves?'

'Ssh!' said the squirrel, in alarm. 'Don't let the goblins hear you. What did the trees say?'

'They said we were to go through the trap-door and up the slippery-slip,' said Joe, in a low voice. 'We can get right up to Moon-Face's then. It's a wonderful idea.'

'Come on then!' said Beth, and the three of them ran to the Faraway Tree, and felt about for the little trap-door. Ooooh! Another adventure!

XXVII. A MOST EXCITING NIGHT

'If only we can creep up the slippery-slip that turns right round and round in the middle of the trunk, and get to Moon-Face's at the top, we shall be able to help him!' said Joe, feeling about for the trap-door.

'I wonder why Moon-Face didn't slip down it himself,' said Beth.

'Oh, he'd think that there would be plenty of red goblins at the bottom of the Tree, ready to catch him when he flew out of the trap-door,' said Joe. 'But I don't believe they know about this slide!'

He found the trap-door and swung it open. 'Hold it open for me whilst I climb in,' he said. Beth held it. Joe began to climb up.

But, dear me, it was most terribly slippery! He simply couldn't manage to get up the slippery-slip at all! As fast as he climbed up a little way he slid down again. He groaned.

'This is awful! We can never get up this way! I shall keep slipping down all the time.'

'Let *me* try!' said Beth eagerly. So Joe slid out of the trap-door and Beth crept in. But it was just the same for her as for Joe. The slide was far too steep and slippery to be climbed.

'Wisha-wisha-wisha!' said the trees nearby. Beth ran to one, put her arms around its trunk, and pressed her left ear to it. She listened.

'Tell the squirrel to go!' whispered the leaves. 'Tell the squirrel to go!'

'Red squirrel, *you* go up!' said Beth at once. 'Can you manage to, do you think?'

'Yes,' said the squirrel. 'I have claws on my feet to hold with, and I am used to climbing. But what's the use of me going? I am not clever enough to make plans with Moon-Face.'

'Wisha-wisha-wisha!' said the trees loudly. Joe pressed his ear to one. 'The squirrel can throw a rope down the slippery-slip!' whispered the tree.

'Of course,' said Joe, in delight. 'Why didn't I think of it?'

'Tell us,' said the girls. Joe told them. 'The squirrel must climb the slide to the top. He must ask Moon-Face for the rope that is let down for the cushions. But instead of letting it down through the branches of the tree, he must let it down through the slide inside. Then we can hang on and be pulled up!'

'Oooh! That's a really good idea,' said Beth.

'Ssh!' said Joe, as he heard a shout from a goblin up the tree. 'We don't want them to guess what we're doing.'

'The goblins are coming down!' whispered Frannie in alarm. 'I can hear them. What shall we do?'

'We'd better get inside the trap-door and sit at the bottom of the slippery-slip as quiet as mice,' whispered Joe. 'Go in first, squirrel, and climb up. You know what to do, don't you?'

'Yes,' said the squirrel, and disappeared up the slide, digging his sharp claws into it just as if he were climbing up the outside of a tree-trunk! Joe pushed

Beth inside and then Frannie. He climbed in himself and shut the trap-door just in time.

Three goblins jumped down to the foot of the tree and began hunting round about. 'I *know* I heard someone!' said one of them.

'Well, so long as we don't let them pass us up the tree, they can't do much!' said another with a laugh. 'I don't think you heard any one – it was just the trees whispering'

'Wisha-wisha-wisha!' said the trees at once.

'There! What did I tell you?' said the goblin. They jumped back into the boughs of the Faraway Tree, and the children hugged one another and chuckled.

'I wonder if the squirrel has got up to the top of the slide yet,' said Joe.

As he spoke a little sound came down the slide – a

soft, slinky sound – and something suddenly touched them!

'Oooh! A snake!' cried Beth in alarm.

'Don't be silly! It's the rope that the good little squirrel has sent down!' said Joe, feeling it. 'Now, we'd better go up one at a time, for Moon-Face will never be able to pull us all up at once.'

Frannie went first. She was hauled all the way up the slide. It was very strange, so dark and quiet. At last she reached the top. Moon-Face was there, red-faced from pulling the rope. A light burned in his funny round room. He was simply over-joyed to see Frannie. He hugged her, and then sent down the rope for Beth. She came up – and then Joe.

'Don't make too much noise,' said Moon-Face in a low voice, as he hugged them all. 'The goblins are outside everyone's door.'

'Oh, Moon-Face, we're so sorry you are captured like this,' said Joe. 'Couldn't you have slid down the slide and escaped? Or did you think there might be goblins at the bottom?'

'Well, I did,' said Moon-Face, 'but I also thought that if I slid down I'd be leaving all my friends behind in the tree, and that seemed a mean thing to do.'

'Yes, it would be rather mean,' said Joe, 'to save yourself and leave the others. Moon-Face, what can we do to help?'

'Well, I simply don't know,' said Moon-Face. 'I've thought and I've thought – but I can't think of anything really good at all.'

'It's a pity Silky isn't here,' said Joe. 'We could talk it all over with her then. She's clever.'

'We can't possibly get to *her*,' said Moon-Face. 'She's locked in, just as I am.'

'Joe! Moon-Face!' said Frannie suddenly, her face red with excitement. 'I've thought of a way to help.'

'What?' cried the others.

'Well – couldn't the red squirrel slip down the slide, out of the trap-door, and take a note to the elves in the wood?' asked Frannie. 'Do you remember how we helped them when we first came to the wood – they said they would always be pleased to help us if we wanted them?'

'Yes – but how could *they* help?' asked Moon-Face doubtfully. Nobody quite knew. But Joe suddenly nodded his head and gave a squeal.

'Ssh!' said everyone at once.

'Sorry,' said Joe, 'but I really have got an idea at last. Listen! The red squirrel can tell the elves to come up here in crowds – we'll pull them up on the rope. Then Moon-Face can shout out to the goblins outside that he'll tell them the magic spells they want to know – and when they open the door the elves and all of us can pour out and overpower the goblins!'

'That's a *splendid* idea!' said Moon-Face, looking at Joe in admiration.

'Simply wonderful!' said the girls. Joe was pleased.

'And we'll unlock everyone's doors and they can all join in!' he said. 'My goodness, this is going to be exciting! Can you see how dreadfully angry the Angry Pixie will be – and Mister Watzisname? Those goblins had better watch out!'

Everyone chuckled. The red squirrel touched Joe's knee. 'Will you give me the note then?' he said. 'I know where Mister Whiskers lives, and I will take the letter to him, and let him call all the elves together.'

Joe took out his pencil and wrote a note on Moon-Face's paper. He folded it and gave it to the red squirrel, who folded it even smaller and tucked it inside his cheek.

'That's in case I'm caught by the goblins,' he said. 'They'll never think of looking for a note inside my cheek!' He sat on his bushy tail, gave himself a push, and set off down the slippery-slip at a tremendous pace.

Frannie giggled. 'His tail is his cushion,' she said. 'Isn't he a darling? I do hope he'll find Mister Whiskers all right.'

'Well, we'd better just sit quietly and wait,' said Moon-Face. 'I don't want the goblins opening my door and seeing you all here. They'll know we've got a plan then.'

'We brought you some of the meal you didn't eat this afternoon,' said Beth, and she unpacked the bag. 'Here are some sandwiches, some cakes, and some toffee.'

'We'll all have some,' said Moon-Face. 'And I've got some Pop Cakes too.'

So they sat round quietly on Moon-Face's curved sofa and bed and chairs, and ate and whispered, waiting for the squirrel to come back with Mister Whiskers and the elves. Whatever would happen then?

XXVIII. THE RED GOBLINS
GET A SHOCK

It seemed a long time before anything happened.
Then Moon-Face pricked up his ears and listened.
'Someone's coming up the slippery-slip,' he said. 'It
must be the little squirrel.'

'I hope it isn't a goblin!' said Frannie, looking
rather scared.

But it was the red squirrel. He hopped out of the
slippery-slip hole and nodded at everyone. 'It's all
right,' he said. 'The elves are coming. I found Mister
Whiskers and he has slipped out to fetch all his family.
There are fifty-one of them!'

'We'd better let the rope down then,' said Moon-
Face, and he let it slither down the slide. Someone
caught hold of it at the other end, and the rope
tightened.

'There's an elf there now!' said Moon-Face, and he
and Joe hauled on the rope. It was heavy. They pulled
and they pulled, panting hard.

'This elf is rather heavy!' said Joe. And no wonder –
for when they at last got the rope to the top, there was
not one elf – but five, hanging on to the rope! They
leapt into Moon-Face's tiny round room, and began
to whisper excitedly. Moon-Face told them all about
the goblins, and they grinned when they heard his
plan.

Down went the rope again, and this time six elves

came up on it. By this time the room was very crowded. But nobody minded.

'We'll have to sit on each other's knees,' said Joe, and giggled at the sight of so many people in Moon-Face's little tree-room.

The elves all looked exactly the same. They all had very long beards, though Mister Whiskers' beard was the longest. It reached right down to his toes.

The rope fetched up all the fifty-one little men, and by that time there was really no room to move! Everyone was excited, and there was such a lot of whispering that it sounded like a thousand leaves rustling at once!

'Now I'm going to bang on the inside of my door and tell the goblins I will let them know the magic spell they want!' said Moon-Face. 'As soon as they open the door you must all rush out and grab hold of them.'

'Wait! I've thought of such a good idea,' said Joe suddenly. 'Let's push them into this room of Moon-Face's – and send someone down the tree to bolt the trap-door – and when they slide down, thinking to escape, they'll all be nicely boxed up in the slide till *we* decide to open the trap-door!'

'That *is* a good idea,' said Mister Whiskers. 'Two elves had better go up the ladder that leads through the clouds, to stop any goblins trying to escape that way – and six of us had better slide down to the foot of the Tree to stop them escaping into the wood.'

Six of the elves at once took cushions and slid down the slippery-slip. They shot out of the trap-door, and bolted it on the outside. They surrounded the foot of the Tree, ready to prevent any naughty goblins from escaping.

The rest of them waited for Moon-Face to speak to the goblins outside. They were all tremendously excited.

Moon-Face banged on the inside of his door. A goblin outside shouted to him:

'Stop that noise!'

'Let me out!' yelled Moon-Face.

'Not till you tell us one of the magic spells you know!' said the goblin.

'I know a spell that will turn people into kings and queens!' shouted Moon-Face.

'Tell us it then,' said the goblin at once.

'Well, open my door,' said Moon-Face. There came the sound of a key turned in a padlock, and then Moon-Face's door was opened. At once the whole crowd of elves poured out like a stream of water! Joe, Beth, and Frannie went out with them, and when the goblins saw the crowd, they gave a yell and leapt down the tree to warn their friends.

Two elves leapt up to the ladder and sat there to prevent any goblins escaping to the land above. Joe, Moon-Face, Beth and Frannie climbed quickly down the tree to let out all the people locked into their homes. How glad everyone was!

Dame Washalot was very angry at being locked in. 'I'll teach those goblins to lock me in!' she shouted. And the old dame picked up her washtub and began to throw water over all the goblins climbing about the tree. What a shock for them! Joe

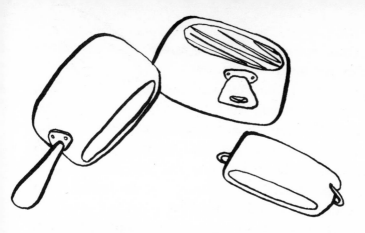

couldn't help laughing.

He unlocked Mister Watzisname's door, and out came Watzisname, shouting and raging, followed by the Saucepan Man. Watzisname chased hard after the terrified goblins!

The Saucepan Man acted in a surprising manner. He took off one saucepan after another, one kettle after another, and threw them after the escaping goblins. Crash! Bang! Clatter!

They let out the Barn Owl, and the three owls that lived together. They flew at the goblins, screeching and hooting. The Angry Pixie was so angry that he flew at Joe when he let him out, and Joe only just explained in time that it was the goblins who were to blame – not him!

Beth let Silky out, but Silky was frightened by all the noise and shouting. Still she managed to catch one goblin by throwing one of her curtains over him. Silky and Beth then took the goblin up the tree and pushed him into Moon-Face's room. When he found the slippery-slip he slid down it in delight, thinking he could escape. But, alas for him, he stopped at the bolted trap-door, and there he stayed, unable to climb up or to get out!

Many other goblins were caught that way too. They tried to escape from the elves by running down the tree to the wood – but when they found six strong elves at the foot they climbed up the tree again to escape into their own land at the top! And then, of course, they found the two elves on the ladder, who pushed them back down again.

So into Moon-Face's house they went, pushed in by Joe, who took great delight in doing so. One by one they tried to escape by sliding down the slippery-slip, and soon the slide was crowded with goblins, piled one on top of the other!

Dawn came, and the sun shone out, lighting up the great branches of the enormous Faraway Tree.

'Now we can see if any goblins are hiding anywhere,' called Moon-Face, who was thoroughly enjoying himself. So he and the elves and Watzisname looked into every hole and corner, behind every branch and tuft of leaves, and pulled out any goblins hidden there. They were marched up to Moon-Face's room, and down the slippery-slip they went. Soon there wasn't a single goblin left. They were all piled on top of one another in the slide, most uncomfortable and upset.

'There!' said Moon-Face at last, pleased with himself and everyone else. 'We've got them all safe. My word, I *am* hungry! What about having a good meal?'

'Look!' called Silky, waving to a lower part of the great tree. 'The Faraway Tree is growing ripe plums just down there! What about having a feast of those?'

'Good!' said Moon-Face. 'Squirrel, go down to the six elves at the foot of the tree and tell them they can come up now. Hey, you two elves on the ladder, you can come down. Silky, can you make us some hot chocolate to drink? Plums and hot chocolate would make a lovely meal.'

Just as they were sitting down to eat and drink, a strange figure came up the tree. He was thin and ragged and knobbly, but his face beamed as if he knew everybody.

'Who's that?' said Frannie at once.

'Don't know,' said Moon-Face, staring.

'I seem to have seen his face before,' said Beth.

'He's a funny-looking creature,' said Joe. 'He looks rather like a scarecrow to me!'

The ragged man came up, and sat down on a branch nearby. He held out his hand for a cup of hot chocolate.

'Who are you?' said Moon-Face.

'What's your name?' asked Silky.

'Play a game?' said the thin man, beaming. 'Yes, certainly – what game shall we play?'

And then everyone knew who it was! It was the Old Saucepan Man – without his kettles and saucepans! He had thrown them all after the goblins, and now he had none left to wear.

'Saucepan! You *do* look different!' said Watzisname, hugging him. 'I didn't know you! Come and have a plum.'

The Saucepan Man looked alarmed. 'Hurt your *thumb*?' he said. 'Oh, I *am* sorry!'

'No, I didn't say I'd hurt my thumb,' said

Watzisname, roaring with laughter, and clapping Saucepan on the back. 'I said, have a *plum*, a *plum*, a *plum*!'

'Thanks,' said the Saucepan Man, and put two large plums in his mouth at once.

'And now,' said Moon-Face, when everyone had finished, 'what about those goblins in the slippery-slip?'

XXIX. THE PUNISHMENT OF THE RED GOBLINS

'It's certainly time we dealt with those red goblins,' said Mister Whiskers, the chief elf, wiping his long beard with a yellow handkerchief. He had dropped plum-juice all down it.

And just at that moment there came a great surprise. A deep voice behind them said 'Oho! Here's a nice little party! What about coming back with me into Wizard Land and doing a few jobs?'

Everyone turned in dismay. They saw a curious figure above them, leaning down from a big branch. It was a wizard, whose green eyes blinked lazily like a cat's.

'It's Mighty-One the Wizard!' said Moon-Face, and he got up to bow, for Mighty-One was as mighty as his name. Everyone did the same.

'Who is he?' whispered Frannie.

'He's the most powerful wizard in the whole world,' whispered back Silky. 'He's come down the ladder – so that means that the Land of Red Goblins has gone and the Land of the Wizards

has come! They are always on the look-out for servants, and I suppose Mighty-One has come down to look for some.'

'Well, *I'm* not going to be a servant to a wizard,' said Frannie.

'You won't be,' said Silky. 'He's not a bad fellow. He

won't take anyone who doesn't want to go. It's good training for a fairy who wants to learn magic.'

Mighty-One blinked his eyes slowly and looked at the little crowd on the branches before him. 'I need about a hundred servants to take back with me,' he said. 'Who will come?'

Nobody said a word. Moon-Face got up and bowed again.

'Your Highness,' he said, 'we none of us want to leave the Enchanted Wood, where we are very happy. You may perhaps find others who would like to go back with you. We beg you not to take any of us.'

'Well,' said the wizard, sliding his green eyes from one person to another, 'I haven't much time. My land will swing away from the Faraway Tree in about an hour. Can you get me the servants I want? If you can, I will not take you.'

Everybody looked worried. But Joe jumped up with a beaming face.

'Your Highness! Would red goblins do for your servants?'

'Excellently,' said Mighty-One. 'They are quick and obedient – but goblins would never agree to coming with me! They belong to their own land.'

Moon-Face, Watzisname, and the Saucepan Man all began to talk at once. Mighty-One lifted up his hand and they stopped. 'One at a time,' said the wizard.

So Moon-Face spoke. 'Sir,' he said, ' we have about a hundred goblins boxed up in the middle of this tree. For a while they held us as prisoners. It would be a very good if you took them away to teach them some discipline and some good manners.'

Mighty-One looked astonished. 'A hundred goblins!!' he said. 'That is very strange. Explain.'

So Moon-Face explained. Mighty-One was most interested to hear of their adventure.

'We'll all go down to the bottom of the tree and let the goblins out one by one,' said Joe, excited. 'Come on! What a shock for them when they see the wizard!'

So they all trooped down the tree in the bright rays of the rising sun. Really, it was all most exciting!

They came to the trap-door at the foot of the tree. Behind it they could hear a lot of shouting and quarelling and pushing.

'Don't push!'

'You're squashing me!'

Moon-Face unbolted the trap-door and opened it. Out shot a red goblin and fell on a green cushion of moss. He picked himself up, blinked in the bright sunlight, and then turned to run. But Mighty-One tapped him with his wand and he stood still. He couldn't move! He looked scared when he saw the wizard.

One by one the red goblins tumbled out of the trap-door, and were tapped by the wizard. Ten, twenty, thirty, forty, fifty, sixty – they came shooting out of the trap-door, surprised and frightened. sliding gradually down the slippery-slip, as one after another slid from the trap-door.

Frannie giggled. It was a funny sight to see.

'It's a very good punishment for those bad goblins,' she said to Silky. 'They came down the ladder to trap *you* and now someone else has trapped *them*, and is taking them back to his land!'

The red goblins stood in a sulky row, quite unable to run away. 'Quick – *march*!' said the wizard, when the last one had slid out of the trap-door – and up the tree went the sulky goblins. It was no use trying to escape. The wizard had put a spell on their legs, and they had to go up to the top of the tree, through the big white cloud and into Wizard Land.

'Just what they deserve,' said Joe. 'My goodness, what an exciting night we've had! I *did* enjoy it.'

'Isn't it cold!' said the Saucepan Man, shivering.

'Cold!' cried Beth and Frannie, who were feeling hot in the morning sun. 'Why, it's as warm as can be.'

'It's because he hasn't got his kettles and saucepans hung around him as usual,' said Watzisname. 'I expect they feel like a coat to him. Poor old Saucepan!'

'I don't like the look of him without his saucepans,' said Frannie. 'He doesn't look right. Can't we collect them for him? They're on the ground – and all about the tree.'

So they began to collect the Saucepan Man's belongings. He was very pleased. They hung his kettles on him, and put his saucepans all round him, with his special one for a hat. Some of them were dented and bent, but he didn't mind a bit.

'There!' said Frannie, pleased. 'You look like yourself now. You looked horrid without all your saucepans on – like a snail without its shell.'

'I never had a bell,' said the Saucepan Man.

'SHELL, I said,' said Frannie.

'Smell?' said the Saucepan

Man, looking round. 'I can't smell anything at the moment. What sort of smell – nice or nasty?'

'*Shell*, not smell,' said Frannie impatiently.

'Oh, *shell*. What shell?' said the Saucepan Man. But Frannie had forgotten what she had said, and she shook her head and laughed. 'Never mind!' she shouted.

'We really must go,' said Joe. 'Mother will be awake now and wondering whatever has happened to us. Oh dear – I do feel sleepy! Come on, girls.'

They said goodbye to all the Tree-dwellers and set off through the Enchanted Wood. Silky went back to her house in the tree, wondering what had happened to her clock, which hadn't joined in the adventure at all. It had been fast asleep.

Moon-Face went back to the tree, yawning. Watzisname and the Saucepan Man climbed back, so tired that they fell fast asleep before they reached their hole, and had to be put safely in the corner of a broad branch by the Angry Pixie, in case they fell down.

Dame Washalot went back, making up her mind to do no washing *that* day. Soon there was peace in the tree, and only the snores of Watzisname could be heard.

Far away up in the tree in the Land of Wizards the red goblins were working hard. Ah – they had got just what they deserved, hadn't they? They wouldn't be in such a hurry to catch other people in future.

The three children got home, and their mother stared at them in surprise.

'You *are* up early this morning,' she said. 'I thought you were still in bed and asleep. Fancy getting up and going out for a walk before breakfast like that.'

How sleepy the children were that day! And, dear me, didn't they go to bed early that night!

'No more wandering through the Enchanted Wood and up the Faraway Tree for me tonight,' said Joe, as he got into bed. 'I vote we don't go there for a long time. It's getting just a bit too exciting.'

But it wasn't long before they went again, as you will see!

XXX. A PLAN FOR BETH'S BIRTHDAY

A week later it was Beth's birthday. She was very excited, because Mother said she could have a small party.

'We'll ask all our friends in the Faraway Tree,' she said.

'Do you really think we should?' said Joe doubtfully. 'I don't think Mother would like Dame Washalot – or Mister Whiskers – or the Angry Pixie.'

'Well, we can't very well ask some and not others,' said Beth. 'The ones we left out would be very hurt indeed.'

'It's awkward,' said Frannie. 'We'd better go and tell Moon-Face and Silky, and ask them what to do.'

But Mother wouldn't let the two girls go off with Joe that day. She said there was a lot of work for them to do in tidying up their room.

'Oh bother!' said Frannie to Joe. 'You'll have to go alone, Joe, and ask Moon-Face and Silky what we ought to do about our party. Don't be too long, or we'll be worried about you. And please don't go climbing up into any strange land without us.'

'Don't worry!' said Joe. 'I'm not going to visit any more lands at the top of the Faraway Tree. I've had enough adventures to last me for the rest of my life!'

He set off. He ran through the Enchanted Wood and came to the Faraway Tree. It was a hot afternoon and not many of the little folk were around.

It seemed almost too hot to climb the tree. Joe whistled. The little red squirrel popped down from the tree and looked at him.

'Leap up to the top of the tree and ask old Moon-Face if he'll drop me down a rope with a cushion on the end, and haul me up, squirrel,' said Joe.

The squirrel bounded lightly up the tree. Soon a rope, with a cushion tied to it, came slipping down the tree. Joe caught hold of it. He sat astride the cushion and tugged the rope. It began to go up the tree, bumping into branches as it went.

It was a funny ride, but Joe enjoyed it. He waved to the Angry Pixie, who was sitting outside his house. He stared at Joe in surprise and then grinned when he saw who it was. The owls were all asleep in their homes. Mister Watzisname was awake for once, and fell out of his chair in alarm when he suddenly saw Joe swinging up through the air, bumping into branches!

When he saw it was Joe, he was so pleased that he fell off his branch on to the Saucepan Man, who was snoozing in a chair just below.

'Ooooouch!' said the Saucepan Man, startled. 'What's the matter? Why are you jumping on me?'

'I'm not,' said Watzisname. 'Look, there's Joe!'

'Go? I don't want to go,' said the Saucepan Man, settling down again. 'Don't be so restless.'

'I said, "There's JOE!"' roared Watzisname.

'Where?' said the Saucepan Man in surprise, looking all round. But by that time, of course, Joe was far away up the Tree, laughing over funny Watzisname and dear old Saucepan!

Watzisname climbed back to his chair and shut his eyes. Soon his snores reached Joe, who was far above, hoping that Silky would see him and go up to Moon-Face's to talk to him. He forgot to look out for Dame Washalot's water, but it missed him nicely, splashing down heavily on poor old Watzisname, making him dream that he was falling out of a boat and into the sea.

Silky did see him, and waved. She climbed the tree quickly to go up to Moon-Face's. By the time she got there Joe had just arrived and was getting off the cushion.

'Hallo!' said Moon-Face and Silky, pleased to see him. 'Where are Beth and Frannie?'

Joe told them. He told them about Beth's birthday too, and her difficulty about how many people she should ask.

'We'd like everyone,' said Joe. 'But Mother wouldn't like some of them, we're sure. What shall we do?'

'I know! I know!' said Silky, clapping her hands suddenly. 'Next week the Land of Birthdays comes to the top of the Faraway Tree – and anyone who has a birthday can go there and give the most wonderful party to all their friends. Oh, it would be lovely! Last time the Birthday Land came, nobody had a birthday, so we couldn't go. But this time we can, because Beth could ask us all!'

'It sounds good,' said Joe. 'But I didn't really want to go into any strange land again, you know. We always seem to get mixed up in odd adventures. So far we've always escaped all right – but we might not another time.'

'Oh, no harm can come to you in the Land of Birthdays!' said Moon-Face, at once. 'It's a wonderful land. You really *must* come! It's a chance you mustn't miss.'

'All right,' said Joe, beginning to feel excited. 'I'll tell the girls when I get back.'

'And we'll tell everyone in the Tree, and Mister Whiskers, and his elves too,' said Silky. 'Beth would like everyone to go, wouldn't she?'

'Oh yes!' said Joe. 'What happens, though? I mean, do we have to arrange for things to eat, or anything? And what about a birthday cake? Frannie was going to make one for Beth.'

'Tell her not to,' said Silky. 'She'll find everything she wants up in the Birthday Land. My word, we *are* lucky! Fancy someone really having a birthday just as the Birthday Land comes along!'

'Beth's birthday is on Wednesday,' said Joe. 'So we'll go up the tree then. I'd better go back and tell the girls now. I said I wouldn't be long.'

'Have a Toffee Shock?' said Moon-Face.

'No, thank you,' said Joe. 'I'd rather have a Pop Cake.'

So they sat and munched the lovely Pop Cakes, and talked about the exciting time they had had with the red goblins.

'Now I really must go,' said Joe, and he got up. He chose a red cushion, said goodbye to Silky and Moon-Face, and shot off down the slippery-

slip. Joe thought he really could do
that all day, it was such a lovely
feeling! He flew out of the trap-door at
the bottom and landed on the moss. He
got up and ran off home.

The girls were pleased to see him back so soon.
When they heard about the Birthday Land they were
tremendously excited.

'Ooooh!' said Beth, going red with joy. 'I am lucky!
I wonder what will happen. Do you suppose there will
be cake for me?'

'Certainly!' said Joe. 'And lots of other things too, I
expect!'

'We shall have to tell Mother,' said Frannie. 'I
wonder if she will let us go.'

Mother didn't seem to mind. 'I expect it's just some
sort of birthday joke your friends in the wood are
playing on you!' she said. 'Yes, you can go, if you like.
Our cottage is really too small for a very large party.'

'I shall wear my best dress,' said Beth happily. 'The
one Mother got me last week, with the blue ribbon!'

But Mother wouldn't let her!

'No,' she said firmly. 'You will all go in your old
clothes. I remember quite well what you looked like
when you went off to see that funny friend of yours,
the Old Saucepan Man. I certainly shall not allow any
of you to wear nice things next Wednesday.'

Beth was nearly in tears. 'But, Mother, I can't go to
my own birthday party in old clothes,' she said.

But it was no good. Mother said they could wear
old clothes or else not go. And that was it.

'I don't know what everyone will think of us, going

to the Birthday Land in our oldest things.' said Joe gloomily. 'I've a good mind not to go.'

But when Wednesday afternoon came, they all thought differently! Old clothes or not, they were going to go!

'Come on!' said Joe. 'It's time we went to the Land of Birthdays!'

XXXI. THE LAND OF BIRTHDAYS

The children set off once again to the Enchanted
Wood. They knew the way to the Faraway Tree very
well by now.

'Wisha-wisha-wisha!' whispered the trees, as the
children ran between them. Beth put her arms round
one, and pressed her left ear to the trunk. 'What
secret are you saying today?' she asked.

'We wish you a happy birthday,' whispered the
leaves. Beth laughed! It was fun to have a birthday!

When they came to the Faraway Tree, how
marvellous it looked! The folk of the tree had bedecked
it with lots of little brightly-coloured flags because it
was Beth's birthday, and it looked simply lovely.

'Oooh!' said Beth, pleased. 'I do feel happy. The
only thing I wish is that I had proper party clothes on,
not my old ones.'

But that couldn't be helped. They were just about
to climb the tree when Dame Washalot's big washing-
basket came bumping down on the end of
Moon-Face's rope for the children to get into.

'Good,' said Joe. 'Get in, girls.' They all got in and
went up the tree at a tremendous rate. 'Moon-Face must
have someone helping him to pull,' said Joe, astonished.

He had. Mister Whiskers was there, with
Watzisname and the Old Saucepan Man, and they
were all pulling like anything. No wonder the basket

shot up the tree!

'Many happy returns of the day,' said everyone, kissing Beth.

'Oh, good! You're not in your best clothes,' said Moon-Face. 'We wondered if you would make it a fancy-dress party, Beth.'

'Oh, I'd love to!' said Beth. 'But we haven't got any fancy dress.'

'We can easily get that in the Birthday Land!' said Silky, clapping her hands for joy. 'Good, good, good! I do like a fancy-dress party!'

'Everybody is ready to go,' said Moon-Face. 'The elves are just below us. Where's Saucepan Man? Hey, Saucepan, where have you got to?'

'He stepped into your slippery-slip by mistake,' said an elf, appearing out of Moon-Face's house. 'He went down the slide with an awful noise. I expect he's at the bottom by now.'

'Good gracious! Just like silly old Saucepan!' said Moon-Face. 'We'd better let down the washing-basket for him, or he'll never get up to us!'

So down went the washing-basket again, and old Saucepan got into it and came up with a clatter of saucepans and kettles.

'Now are we really all ready?' said Moon-Face. 'Silky – Watzisname – Saucepan – the Angry Pixie – Dame Washalot – Mister Whiskers – the elves....'

'Goodness! What a lovely lot of people are coming!' said Beth, seeing all the elves and tree-folk on the branches below. 'Is that Dame Washalot? What a nice old woman!'

Dame Washalot was beaming happily. For once she

was going to leave her wash-tub. Going to the Land of Birthdays was not a treat to be missed!

'Come on, then,' said Moon-Face, and he led the way up the ladder. Up he went, popped his head above to make quite sure that the Land of Birthdays was there, and then jumped straight into it!

Everyone climbed up. 'That's all, I think,' said Moon-Face, peering down. 'Oh no – there's someone else. Whoever is it? I thought we were all here?'

'Goodness! It's my clock!' said Silky. 'The one I got in the Land of Take-What-You-Want!'

Sure enough, it was. 'Ding-dong-ding-dong!' it cried indignantly, as it climbed up on its flat feet.

'All right, all right, we'll wait for you!' said Silky. 'Go carefully up the ladder. You weren't really asked, you know.'

'Oh, I'd love your clock to come to my party,' said Beth at once. 'Come along, clock.'

'Ding-dong,' said the clock, pleased, and managed

to get up the ladder.

The Land of Birthdays was simply beautiful. To begin with, there was always birthday weather there – brilliant sunshine, blue sky, and a nice little breeze. The trees were always green, and there were always daisies and buttercups growing in the fields.

'Oh, it's lovely, it's lovely!' cried Beth, dancing around joyfully. 'Moon-Face, what about our fancy-dress? Where do we get that?'

'Oh, you'll find everything in that house over there,' said Moon-Face, pointing to a very pretty house. They all trooped over to it. As they went, small brown rabbits hopped out of holes, called 'A Happy Birthday!' to Beth, and popped back inside. It was all very exciting.

Everyone crowded into the pretty house. It was full of cupboards – and in the cupboards were the most thrilling costumes you can think of.

'Oh, look at this!' cried Joe, in delight, as he came across a sailor's outfit, with a smart hat that had blue, white and gold on it, just like the captain of a ship. 'Just the right size for me!'

He put it on. Beth chose a dress like a fairy's, and Frannie chose a clown's costume with a pointed hat. She looked just like the real thing.

Moon-Face dressed up as a pirate and Silky became a daffodil. Watzisname was a policeman, and as for the Old Saucepan Man, he simply could *not* find a costume to fit him, because he was so bumpy with kettles and saucepans!

Everyone else dressed up and, oh my, they did look convincing! Beth had wings with her dress, but she was disappointed because she couldn't fly with them. How she would have loved to spread her wings and fly, as the real fairies did!

'Now for balloons!' said Silky, and she danced into the sunshine and ran to an old balloon-seller who was sitting surrounded by a great cloud of coloured balloons. Everybody chose one, and what games they had!

Suddenly a bell rang, and Moon-Face gave a shout of joy.

'Birthday feast! Come on, everyone!'

He rushed to a long, long table set out in the field. Beth ran with the others, and took her place at the head of the table. But to her great surprise and disappointment there was no food on the table at all – just empty plates, cups, and glasses!

'Don't look so upset!' whispered Silky. 'You've got to *wish* your own birthday feast!'

Beth gave a squeak. *Wish* her own birthday feast! Oooh! That would be the best fun in the world!

'Don't wish for bread and butter!' called Moon-Face. 'Wish for an ice-cream sundae, I like those!'

'I wish for an ice-cream sundae!' said Beth at once. And immediately the biggest, tallest sundae you ever saw appeared on one of the empty plates. Moon-Face helped himself.

'Wish for strawberries and vanilla ice-cream!' cried Frannie, who simply loved that.

'I wish for strawberries and vanilla ice-cream!' said Beth, and an enormous dish of strawberries appeared, with a large tub of vanilla ice-cream beside it. 'And I wish for chocolate cake too – and lemonade – and – and – and...'

'Fruit salad!' yelled someone.

'Doughnuts!' cried Watzisname.

'Cheese sandwiches!' begged Mister Whiskers.

'Ding-dong-ding-dong!' said Silky's clock in the greatest excitement. Everyone laughed.

'Don't wish for ding-dongs!' said Joe. 'We've got plenty of those, as long as Silky's clock is here!'

The clock chimed fourteen without stopping. It wandered about, looking as happy as could be.

Everyone began to eat. My goodness, it was a wonderful feast! The strawberries and vanilla ice-cream and the sundae went almost at once, for Mister Whiskers and fifty elves decided that they liked those very much too! So Beth had to wish for some more.

'What about my birthday cake?' she asked Silky. 'Do I wish for that too?'

'No, it just comes,' said Silky. 'It will appear right in the middle of the table. You just watch.'

Beth watched. There was a wonderful silver dish in the middle of the table. Something seemed to be forming there. A curious sort of mist hung over it.

'The birthday cake is coming!' shouted Joe, and everyone watched the silver dish. Gradually a great cake shaped itself there – oh, a wonderful cake, with red, pink, white, and yellow decorations made from sugar, and shaped like little flowers. On the top were eight candles burning, for Beth was eight that day. Her name was written in big sugar letters on the top: 'BETH. A VERY HAPPY BIRTHDAY!'

Beth felt very proud. She had to cut the cake, of course. It was quite a difficult job, for there were so many people to cut a slice for.

'This is a wishing-cake!' said Moon-Face, when everyone had a piece on their plate. 'So wish, wish, wish, when you eat it – and your wish will come true!'

The children stared at him in delight. What should they wish? Frannie was just holding her cake in her hand, thinking of a wish, when the Old Saucepan Man upset everything! Whatever do you think he did?

XXXII. THE LITTLE LOST ISLAND

'Wouldn't you like to wish?' said Moon-Face, turning to the Old Saucepan Man, who was just about to bite into his cake.

'Fish?' said the Saucepan Man, in delight. 'Yes, I'd love to fish! I wish we were all fishing for fine fat fishes in the middle of the sea.'

Well! What a wish to make, just as he was eating a wishing-cake, for he hadn't heard Moon-Face properly.

Anyway, the wish immediately came true. A wind blew down, and lifted up the whole crowd of guests at the table. Sitting on their chairs, clinging tightly, they flew through the air for miles!

Whatever was happening?

Down flew the chairs in the big wind. A shower of salt spray drenched everyone. Joe gasped and looked down. Bump! He and everyone else landed on soft sand, rolled off their chairs, and sat up, blinking in surprise.

The long-bearded elves looked frightened. Moon-Face kept opening and shutting his mouth like a fish, he was so astonished. Joe was cross, and so was the Angry Pixie.

'*Now* what's happened?' said Dame Washalot, in a most annoyed voice. 'Why have we come here?'

'Look at all those fishing-rods!' said Silky, pointing to a whole row of rods standing in the sand, with their fishing lines in the water.

'Waiting for *us*!' groaned Moon-Face. 'Silly old Saucepan Man didn't hear what I said about wishing – he thought I said *fishing* – and he wished us all here, fishing in the sea!'

'Goodness!' said Beth, alarmed. 'Where are we, then?'

'I think we're on the Little Lost Island,' said Silky, looking round. 'It's a funny little place, always floating about and getting lost. But there's always good fishing to be had from it.'

'Fishing!' said Joe, in disgust. 'Who wants to go fishing in the middle of a birthday party? Let's get back at once.'

'Ding-dong-ding-dong!' said Silky's clock, walking about at the edge of the sea and getting its feet wet in the waves.

'Come back, clock!' called Silky. 'You know you can't swim.'

The clock came back and wiped its feet on the grass that grew around. Beth thought it was a remarkably sensible clock, and she wished she had one like it.

'You know, we really must do something about getting back to the Land of Birthdays,' said Joe, getting up and looking around the little island. 'What can we do? Is there a boat here?'

There was nothing except the fishing-rods! Nobody even touched them, for they didn't feel in the least like fishing. The Little Lost Island was just a hilly stretch of green grass and nothing else whatsoever.

'I really don't know *what* to do!' said Moon-Face, frowning. 'Do you, Mister Whiskers?'

Mister Whiskers was dressed up like Santa Claus, and looked very fine indeed, with his long beard. He rubbed his nose thoughtfully and shook his head.

'The difficulty is,' he said, 'that none of us has any magic with him, because we're all in fancy-dress and our other clothes are in the Land of Birthdays. So the spells and magic we keep in our pockets are not here.'

'Well, we shan't starve,' said Watzisname. 'We can always fish.'

'Fancy eating fish and nothing but fish always!' said Joe, making a face. 'When I think of all those lovely things that Beth wished for – and nobody to eat them now! Really, I could cry!'

Frannie had something in her hand and she looked down to see what it was. It was a piece of the birthday cake. Good! She could eat that, at any rate. She lifted the delicious cake to her mouth and took a nibble.

'What are you eating?' asked Moon-Face, bending over to see.

'A bit of the birthday cake,' said Frannie, cramming all of it into her mouth.

'Don't eat it! Don't swallow it!' yelled Moon-Face suddenly, dancing round Frannie as if he had gone quite mad. 'Stop! Don't swallow!'

Frannie stared at him in astonishment. So did everyone else.

'What's gone wrong with Moon-Face?' asked Silky anxiously. Frannie stood still with her mouth full of birthday cake, looking with amazement at Moon-Face.

'What's the matter?' she asked with her mouth full.

'You've got a bit of the wishing-cake in your mouth, Frannie!' shouted Moon-Face, hopping first on one leg and then on the other. 'Wish, dear girl, wish!'

'What shall I wish?' said Frannie.

'Wish us back to the Land of Birthdays, of course!' yelled everyone in excitement.

'Oh,' said Frannie, 'I didn't think of that! I wish we were all back in the Land of Birthdays, enjoying our feast!'

Darkness fell round everyone very suddenly. No wind came this time. Moon-Face put out his hand and took Silky's. What was happening?

Then daylight came back again – and everyone gave a shout of surprise and delight. They were back in the Land of Birthdays! Yes – there was the table in front of them and more chairs to sit down on, and the same delicious food as before!

'Oh, good, good, good!' shouted everyone, and sat down at once. They beamed at one another, very thankful to be back from the Little Lost Island.

'What a strange little adventure!' said Joe, helping himself to a large piece of wishing-cake. 'Please be careful what you wish, everybody – we don't want any more adventures like that in the middle of a party!'

'I wish that my wings could fly!' said Beth, as she munched her cake. And at once her silver wings spread themselves out, and she rose into the air like a big butterfly, flying beautifully. Oh, it was the loveliest feeling in the world!

'Look at me – look at me!' she cried – and everyone looked. Frannie called out to her. 'Don't fly too far,

Beth. Don't fly too far!'

Beth soon flew down to the table again, her cheeks red with excitement and joy. This was the loveliest birthday party she had ever had!

Everybody wished their wishes except the Old Saucepan Man, who had already wasted his. Frannie, too, had wished her wish when she was on the Little Lost Island, but when she looked upset because she had lost her wish, Moon-Face whispered to her.

'Don't be upset. Tell me what you really wanted to wish and I'll wish it for you. I don't want a wish for myself.'

'Oh, Moon-Face, you *are* kind!' said Frannie. 'Well, if you really mean it, I did want a doll that could walk and talk.'

'Easy!' said Moon-Face at once. 'I wish that Frannie had a doll that walks and talks.'

And at that very moment Silky cried out in wonder and pointed behind her. Everyone looked. Coming along on small, plump legs was a doll, beautifully dressed in blue, with a bag in its hand. It walked to Frannie and looked up at her.

'Oh! You lovely, beautiful doll!' cried Frannie in the greatest delight, and she lifted the doll on to her knee. It cuddled up to her and said, 'I belong to you. I am your own doll. My name is Peronel.'

'What a sweet name!' said Frannie, hugging the doll. 'What have you got in that bag, Peronel?'

'All my other clothes,' said the doll, and opened her bag. Inside were nightdresses, a dressing-gown, an overcoat, a raincoat, overalls, dresses, and all kinds of other clothes. Frannie was simply delighted.

'What did you wish, Joe?' asked Beth. Joe was looking all round and about as if he expected something to arrive at any moment.

'I wished for a pony of my own,' said Joe. 'Oh! Look! Here it comes! What a beauty!'

A little black pony, with a white mark on its forehead and four white feet, came trotting up to the party. It went straight to Joe.

'My own little pony!' cried the little boy, in delight. 'Let me ride you! I shall call you Midnight Star – for the little white star on your black coat.'

He jumped on the pony's back and together they went galloping round the Land of Birthdays.

'Now let's play games!' cried Moon-Face, capering about. And as soon as he said that, the table vanished and music began to play.

'Musical chairs! Musical chairs!' shouted Silky, as the chairs suddenly put themselves together in a long row. 'Come on, everybody!'

XXXIII. SAFE BACK HOME AGAIN – AND GOOD-BYE!

The party went on and on. The game of musical chairs was fun, for instead of somebody taking a chair away each time the music stopped, the chair took itself away, walked neatly off, and stood watching.

Silky won that game. She was so quick and light on her feet. A big box of chocolates came flying down through the air to her, when she sat down on the very last chair and pushed Moon-Face away! She was delighted.

'Let's all have one!' she said, and opened the box at once. Whilst they were eating they saw a most astonishing sight.

'Look!' said Moon-Face, almost swallowing his chocolate in astonishment. 'What's this coming?'

Everyone looked. It seemed like a lot of little brightly coloured men, running very upright. What do you suppose they were?

'Birthday presents!' shouted Watzisname, jumping off his seat in delight. 'Presents – running to us – ready to be unwrapped!'

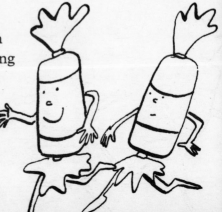

Really, those presents were the greatest fun! They were like little gift-wrapped boxes on tiny legs, dodging away, trying not to be caught! Everyone ran after them, laughing and shouting. One by one the happy little boxes were caught, and then they were unwrapped and opened. My goodness, what special things there were inside!

'I've got a brooch in the shape of the Faraway Tree!' cried Frannie, pinning it on herself.

'I want one too,' said her doll.

'Well, you must catch a present then, Peronel,' said Frannie, and how she laughed to see her doll running about after a red birthday-present box! Peronel caught one at last and brought it back to Frannie. Inside there was a teddy-bear shaped brooch, which Peronel was simply delighted with!

Joe found a shining silver whistle inside his present. When he blew it sounded just like all the birds in the Enchanted Wood. He was very happy with it. Moon-Face found a special squeaker that sounded just like a cat mewing, and made the Old Saucepan Man go hunting for cats all the time! Naughty Moon-Face! He pressed his squeaker behind the Saucepan Man and laughed till he cried to hear him calling, 'Puss! Puss! Puss!' and looking under tables and chairs.

Silky's clock wanted a present too. So it ran after one, and trod on one to catch it. It held it with its foot and unwrapped it with Silky. What do you suppose was in it? A tiny can of oil!

'Just the thing to oil your clockwork wheels and springs with!' said Silky in delight. The clock was very pleased. It chimed twenty-two times without stopping, much to the walking doll's astonishment.

They played hide-and-seek, and immediately the most exciting bushes and trees sprang up everywhere to hide behind. Really, the Birthday Land was the most exciting country to be in!

Then they played pin-the-tail-on-the-donkey – and a giant toy donkey and a big fluffy tail appeared out of nowhere!

Then they thought they would have races – and, hey presto – they saw a crowd of small cars drive up, all ready to be raced! In got everyone, choosing the car they liked best. There was even a tiny one for Peronel the doll, and an extra one for Silky's clock, who joined in the fun and ding-donged merrily all the time.

The Old Saucepan Man won the race, though he dropped a few saucepans on the way. Moon-Face handed him a box of toffee that had appeared for the winner.

'You've won!' he said.

'Run?' said the Saucepan Man. 'All right, I'll run!' And he ran and ran, just to show how fast he could run when he wanted to. What a noise he made, with his kettles and saucepans clattering all round him!

'Supper-time, supper-time!' shouted Moon-Face

suddenly, and he pointed to a lovely sight. About a hundred toadstools had suddenly grown up, and appearing on them were jugs of all kinds of delicious drinks, and cakes and fruit. Smaller toadstools grew beside the big ones.

'They are for seats!' cried Silky, sitting down on one and helping herself to some acornade. 'I'm hungry! Come on, everyone!'

Beth flew down from the air. She *did* love flying. Frannie ran up with her doll, who followed her everywhere, talking in her little high voice. Joe galloped up on his pony. Everyone was very happy.

It began to get dark, but nobody minded, because big lanterns suddenly shone out everywhere in the trees and bushes. As they sat and ate, there came a loud bang-bang!

Peronel cuddled up to Frannie, frightened. Silky's clock tried to get on Silky's knee, scared, but she pushed it off.

'What's that?' said Joe, patting his frightened pony.

'Fireworks! Fireworks!' shouted the Angry Pixie in delight. 'Look! Look!'

And there, in front of them, were the fireworks, setting themselves off beautifully. Rockets flew high and sizzled down in coloured stars. Firework wheels whizzed round and round. Firecrackers popped and banged and jumped around. It was splendid to watch!

'This is the loveliest birthday party I've ever heard of,' said Beth happily, flapping her big wings, as she sat and watched the fireworks. 'Lovely things to eat – wishes that come true – exciting games – splendid presents – and now fireworks.'

'We have to go home at midnight,' said Moon-Face, pushing away Silky's clock, which was trying to sit on his toadstool with him.

'How shall we know when it's midnight?' asked Frannie, thinking that it really was time her doll went to bed.

They knew all right – because when midnight came Silky's clock stood up and chimed loudly, twelve times – Dong-dong-dong-dong-dong-dong-dong-dong-dong-dong-dong-dong!

'To the ladder! To the ladder!' cried Moon-Face, hurrying everyone there. 'The Birthday Land will soon be on the move!'

The ladder was there. Everyone climbed down it and called goodbye. The elves took cushions and slid off down the slippery-slip. Mister Whiskers got his beard caught round one of the legs of Moon-Face's sofa and nearly took that with him down the slide. Moon-Face just stopped it in time, and unwound his beard.

'What about my pony?' asked Joe anxiously. 'Do you suppose he will mind sliding down, Moon-Face?'

'Well, he can't climb down the tree, and he certainly wouldn't like going down in the washing-basket,' said Moon-Face. So they sat the surprised pony on a cushion and he slid down in the greatest astonishment, wondering what in the world was happening to him!

Frannie slid down with her sleepy doll on her knee. Beth carefully took off her wings and folded them up. She didn't want to have them spoilt. She wanted to use them every day. She was very proud of them.

The pony arrived on the cushion of moss quite safely. Joe mounted him. It was dark in the wood, but the moon was just rising, and they would be able to see their way home quite well.

'Goodbye!' called Moon-Face from the top of the tree. 'We've had a lovely time!'

'Goodbye!' called Silky. 'Ding-dong!' said her clock sleepily.

'Take care of yourselves!' shouted Watzisname.

Moon-Face pressed his squeaker loudly, and then giggled to hear the Saucepan Man call, 'Puss! Puss! Puss! Wherever *is* that cat!'

Slishy-sloshy-slishy-sloshy! Good gracious, was that Dame Washalot doing washing already? Joe dodged away on his pony and the girls ran from the tree. Mister Whiskers got the water all over him, for he was standing nearby, and he was most upset.

'Come on, girls!' said Joe, laughing. 'We really *must* go home! We shall never wake up in the morning!'

So they went home once more, through the Enchanted Wood, with the moon shining pale and cold between the trees.

'Wisha-wisha-wisha!' whispered the leaves.

Joe put his pony into the field outside the cottage. Frannie undressed Peronel and put her into her doll's bed. Beth put her wings carefully into a drawer. They all undressed and got sleepily into bed.

'Goodnight!' they said. 'What a lovely day it's been. We *are* lucky to live near the Enchanted Wood!'

They were, weren't they? Perhaps they will have more adventures one day; but now we must say goodbye to them, and leave them fast asleep,

dreaming of the Land of Birthdays, and all the lovely
things that happened there!

THE END